BIG IDEAS
THAT CHANGED THE WORLD

WE THE PEOPLE!

DON BROWN

AMULET BOOKS · NEW YORK

Using a hand-drawn template as a guide, all lines, colors,
and textures were created digitally.

Cataloging-in-Publication Data has been applied for and may be obtained
from the Library of Congress.

ISBN 978-1-4197-5738-9

Text and illustrations copyright © 2022 Don Brown
Edited by Howard W. Reeves
Book design by Chelsea Hunter

Published in 2022 by Amulet Books, an imprint of ABRAMS. All rights reserved.
No portion of this book may be reproduced, stored in a retrieval system, or
transmitted in any form or by any means, mechanical, electronic, photocopying,
recording, or otherwise, without written permission from the publisher.

Printed and bound in Thailand

10 9 8 7 6 5 4 3 2 1

Amulet Books are available at special discounts when
purchased in quantity for premiums and promotions as well as fundraising
or educational use. Special editions can also be created to specification.
For details, contact specialsales@abramsbooks.com or the address below.

Amulet Books® is a registered trademark of Harry N. Abrams, Inc.

ABRAMS The Art of Books
195 Broadway, New York, NY 10007
abramsbooks.com

Dedicated to Lorraine, Evan, and Ike

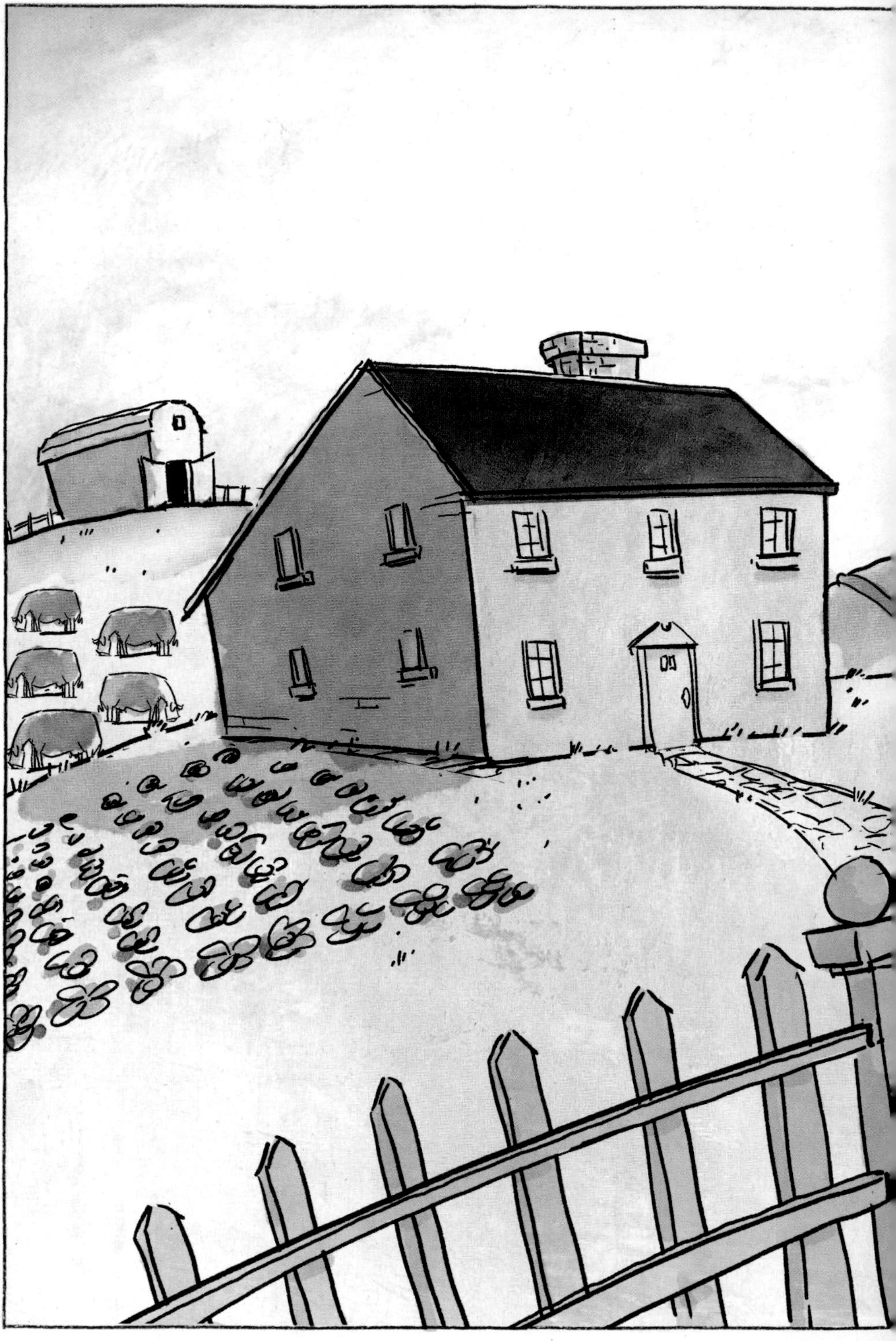

Beautiful, isn't it?
This is John's and my farm. But my husband, John—Founding Father John Adams, that is—was absent a lot, thumbing his nose at the king of England and helping invent these United States of America. I then was responsible for the farm, planting and harvesting crops and tending livestock. I was in charge, the leader of the family, farmhands, and staff.

There are leaders, everywhere . . . at work, at school, and at home. The leaders of countries have different titles; some are called premiers, prime ministers, or presidents. Some seized the job, others inherited it, while others earned it. Some lead alone and can't be second-guessed; others share leadership, while still others lead based on established rules.

The hows and whys of all the different kinds of leadership is the story of government. It's a Big Idea that's very old.

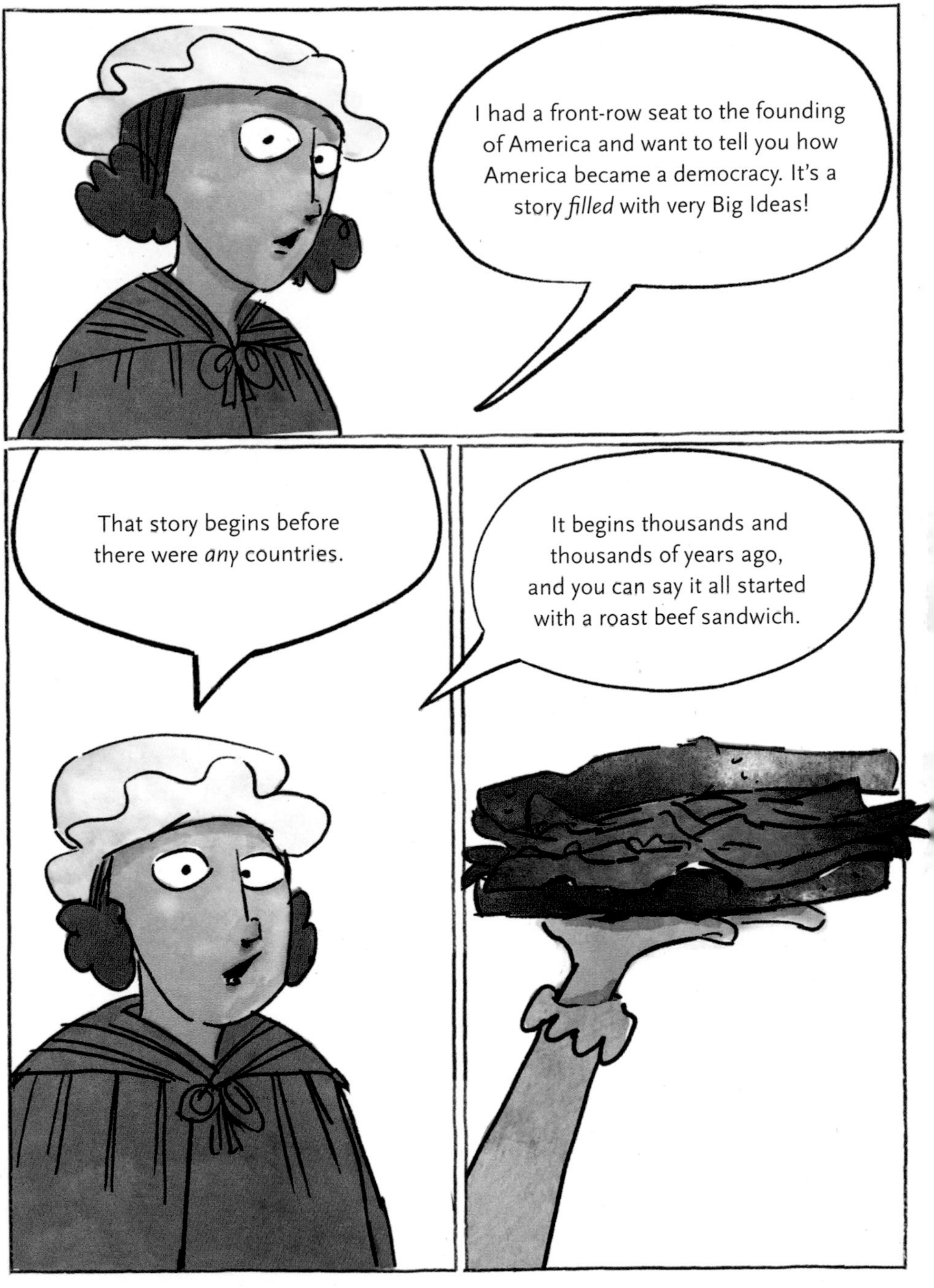
I had a front-row seat to the founding of America and want to tell you how America became a democracy. It's a story *filled* with very Big Ideas!
That story begins before there were *any* countries.
It begins thousands and thousands of years ago, and you can say it all started with a roast beef sandwich.

Yes, I know that sounds silly but consider how a roast beef sandwich is made . . . with bread . . . with beef.

The bread comes from wheat, a grain that needs to be planted, its seeds harvested, milled, and baked.

The beef is a product of cows, an animal that needs to be bred, fed, and slaughtered.

These are tasks that weren't called for about one hundred forty thousand years ago, when early people survived on a diet without beef sandwiches, instead eating what could be gathered—seeds, nuts, roots, fruits, and such—or hunted or fished.

But when people began growing edible plants and raising animals about twelve thousand years ago, they discovered these more complicated tasks were best accomplished when someone was in charge to assign them and ensure the work was done. To put it simply, when people began to rely on farming for food, they had to decide whether to have someone in charge and eat or have no one in charge and starve.

And so, leaders emerged to lead the people and organize things, like growing food. And eventually towns or villages emerged. And leaders ruled them as well.

Who the first leaders were and how they rose to power is lost to time. But, given the history of what followed, it's likely they were men who used violence or threats of violence to grab power.

As one wise observer said of early leaders, "could we . . . trace them . . . we'd find . . . them nothing better than the principal ruffian of some restless gang."

The ruffians' power grew, first over their neighbors and then far beyond them. They found a title—such as *King, Emperor, Mogul, Your Majesty,* or some such thing—and claimed lifelong, absolute power . . . which would then be passed on to their sons at the time of death.

But what about women? Wives and daughters? Except for a few notable exceptions over the centuries, it was men who ruled.

Ugh. "All men would be tyrants if they could!"

About five thousand years ago, towns and cities began to be gathered together into realms or kingdoms. Some grew to enormous size known as *empires*. And empires rose and fell. And mostly all were ruled by one man who held absolute power.

Ideas about how to rule evolved. Rules were set down.

About 1750 BCE, Hammurabi's Code, named after a Babylonian king, became one of the first written collections of laws, outlining crimes and their punishments.

"If a man puts out the eye of another man, his eye shall be put out."
"If a man knocks out the teeth of his equal, his teeth shall be knocked out."

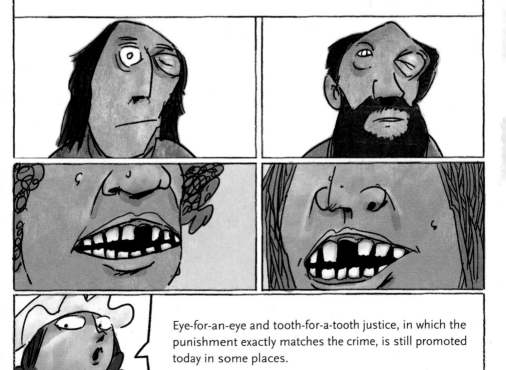

Eye-for-an-eye and tooth-for-a-tooth justice, in which the punishment exactly matches the crime, is still promoted today in some places.

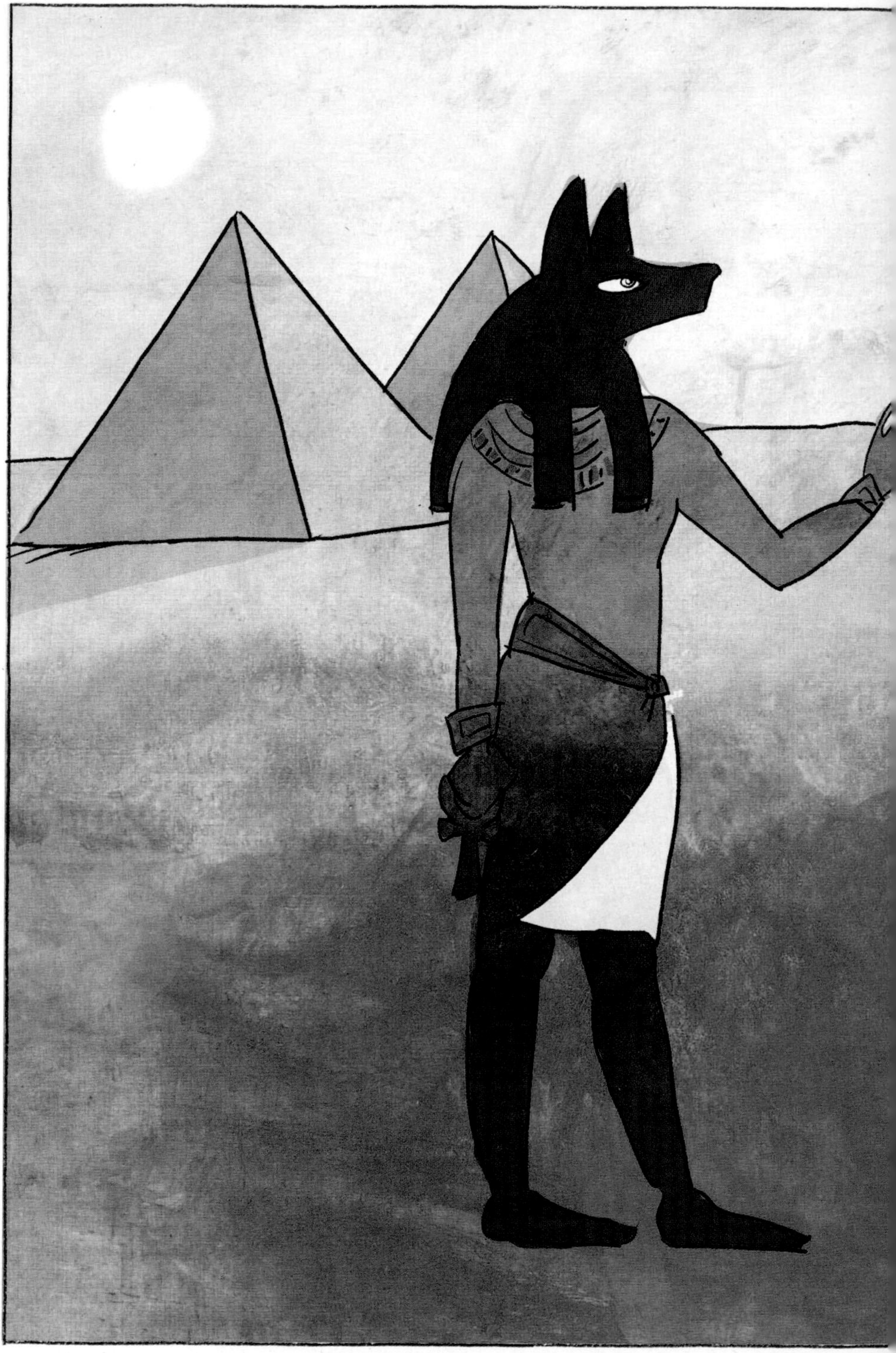

Some of the all-powerful kings boasted of being the agents of the gods. Some—like the pharaohs, the kings, and occasional queens of Egypt—claimed to *be* gods.

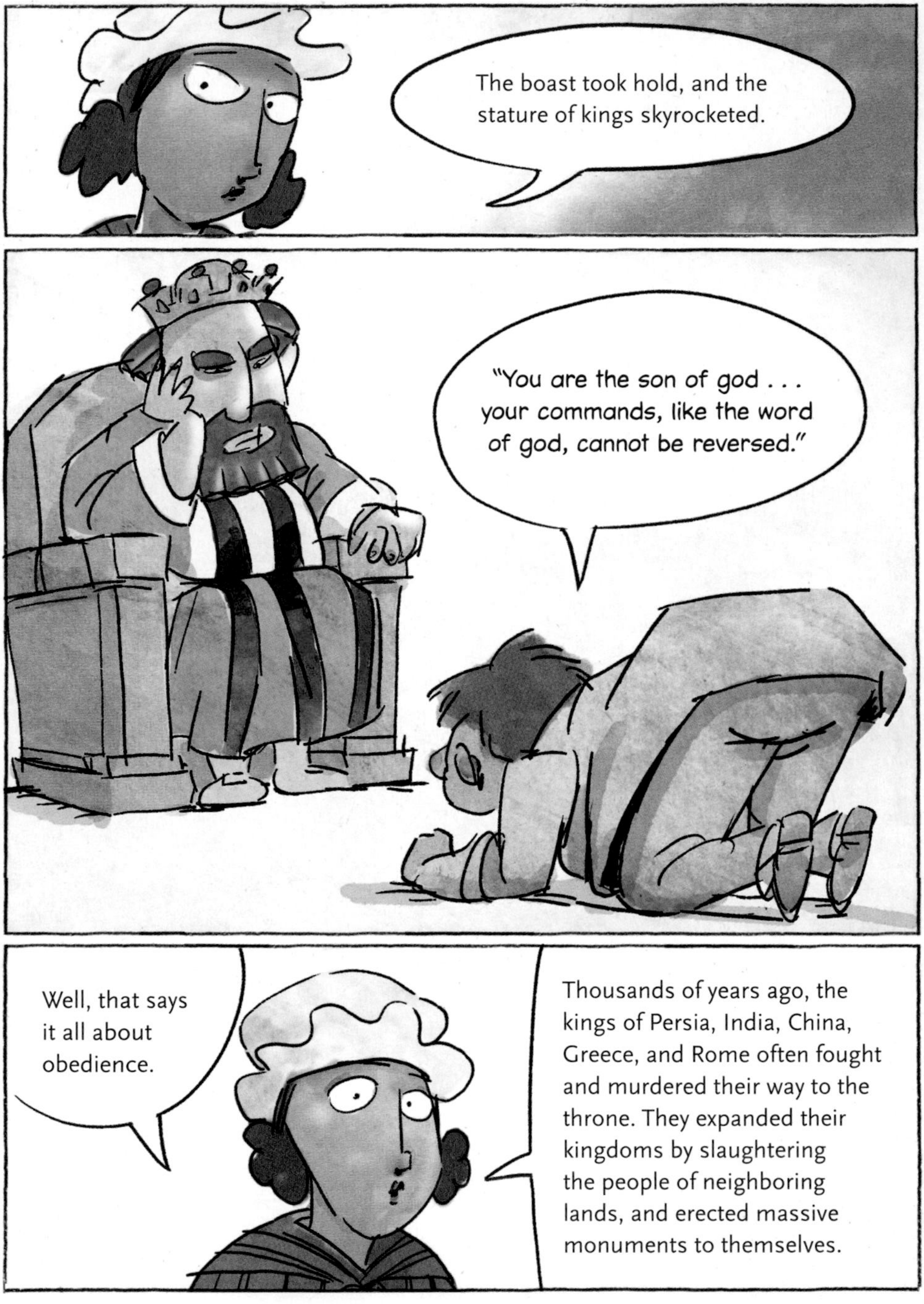
The boast took hold, and the stature of kings skyrocketed.
"You are the son of god . . . your commands, like the word of god, cannot be reversed."
Well, that says it all about obedience.
Thousands of years ago, the kings of Persia, India, China, Greece, and Rome often fought and murdered their way to the throne. They expanded their kingdoms by slaughtering the people of neighboring lands, and erected massive monuments to themselves.

Was monarchy—the absolute rule by kings and, sometimes, queens—the only government people could expect?

No . . .

a few corners of the world had no kings. Such a place is called a republic.

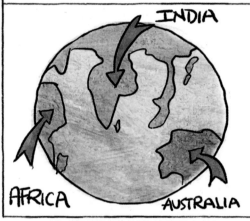

INDIA

AFRICA

AUSTRALIA

About twenty-seven hundred years ago, some ancient parts of India were republics, employing special gatherings of wealthy, powerful elites, or assemblies, to choose rulers. Although the assemblies excluded ordinary people, they still prevented leaders from having king-like power.

In Greece a new kind of republic appeared in the fourth and fifth centuries BCE. The king of the city of Athens was toppled and replaced with *demokratia*, which means "people power" or "rule by the people."

We know it as democracy.

It "favors the many instead of the few."

"The basis of a democratic state is liberty."

It was a "direct" democracy: Citizens of Athens gathered together to vote for or against proposed laws. But I should add, not *all* citizens—only males over eighteen years old. Athenian democracy seems to have been as off-limits to women as was a monarchy.

The day-to-day operation of the city was run by citizens chosen by lottery.

A pool of citizen jurors ran the courts.

Democratic Athens lasted for about two hundred years. But in the end, Athens was conquered by a neighboring king and returned to monarchy.

About 509 BCE, another city also grew in size and power . . . Rome, Italy. Its citizens, too, tossed out a bad king and became a republic.

*ROMANS DIDN'T HAVE SUITCASES.

In the king's place were two consuls—men—who each had power to cancel the orders of the other and prevent either from seizing kingly powers. New consuls were elected each year . . . by men. Of course.

I'M RIGHT!

I'M RIGHT!

The consuls were advised by a senate, a group of rich . . . men.

I might as well tell you now that excluding women from exercising power was a routine practice for thousands of years. More care should have been given!

The wealthy class, called the patricians, kept a tight hold on Rome until violent protest allowed ordinary people, the plebeians, to have a share of power. The plebeians had their own assemblies that also elected two tribunes who helped run Rome.

CONSUL CONSUL TRIBUNE TRIBUNE

This arrangement went on for about five hundred years until it was upended by the ambitions of a few men. The most famous of them, Julius Caesar, was murdered by the senate out of fear he'd make himself king.

Julius Caesar

Despite ridding Rome of Caesar, the region would be ruled for about the next five hundred years by a series of emperors with sweeping powers approved by the gods, or at least that's how the emperors explained it.

Rome wasn't the only great empire.

In about 247 BCE, Qin Shi Huang declared himself China's first emperor after uniting a helter-skelter of small kingdoms into a single dynasty or kingdom.

In West Africa, Sundiata Keita, the Lion King, founded the gold-rich Mali Empire around 1235 CE.

In South America in the early 1500s, Montezuma ruled the Aztec Empire, including its sprawling capital of Tenochtitlan.

In Arabia the birth of the religion of Islam around 600 CE brought a series of vast empires stretching from Europe to Asia. They were headed by caliphates who ruled over both religious and government matters. This is called a theocracy.

The Roman pope in Italy also had both Christian and government powers. For example, Pope Urban II launched the First Crusade in 1095 CE, sending thousands of Christians to battle Muslims in the Middle East.

"It is the will of God!"

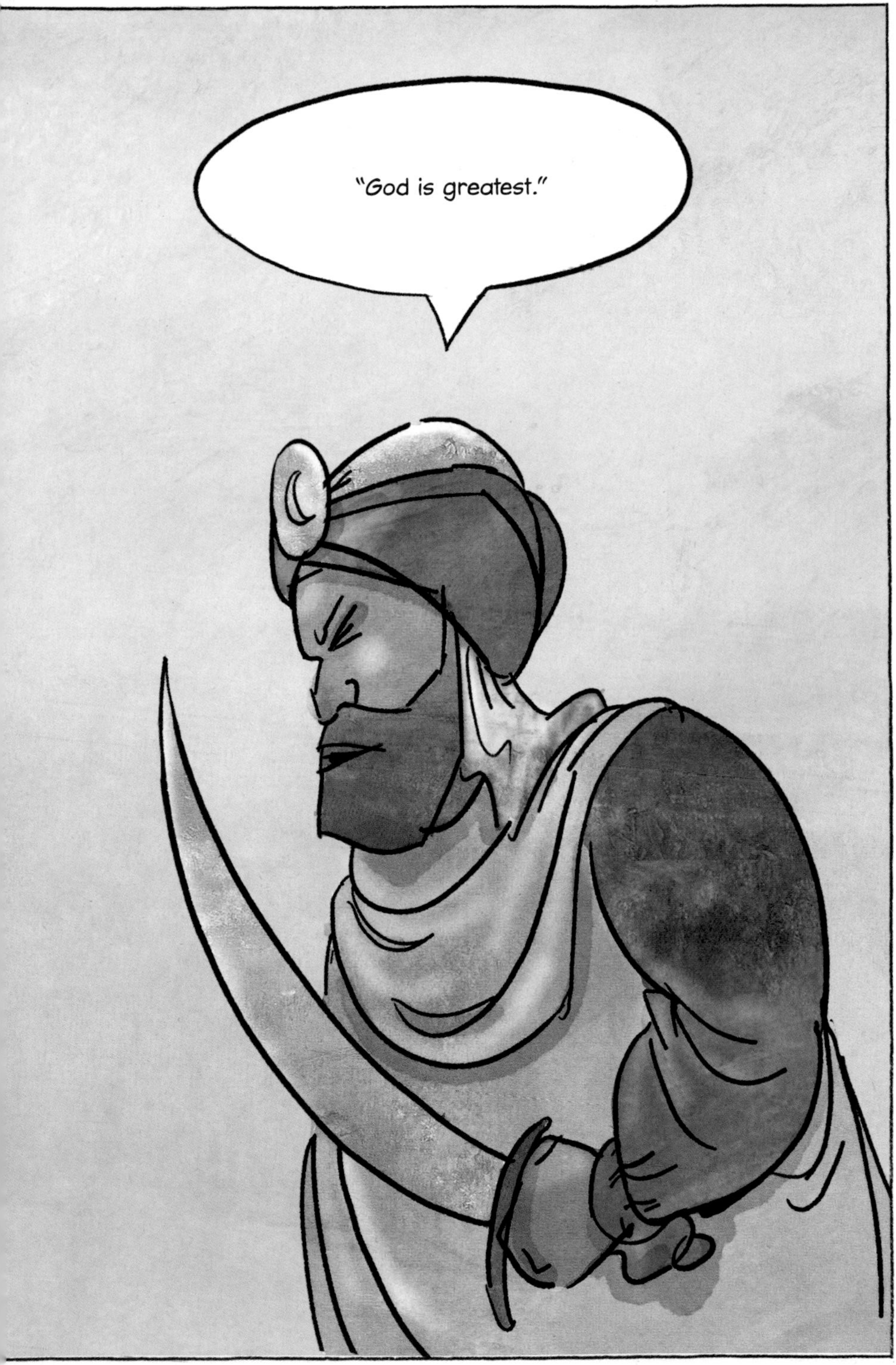
"God is greatest."

In 1215, English King John found himself in a mess.

He'd quarreled with the Pope, lost a war with France . . .

risked losing his crown to opponents, and was nearly broke.

When he tried to muscle English nobles into refilling the royal treasury, a civil war broke out. Faced with being thrown off his throne, he made a deal. We know it as the Magna Carta.

The Magna Carta limited the king's power so that it wasn't *absolute*, or unchecked.

It set down sixty-three clauses, or rules, for the king to obey.

Some of the Magna Carta's Big Ideas still apply to many governments today, like the rule that a person can't be imprisoned or dispossessed, or exiled, or in any way punished . . . except by the lawful judgment of their peers . . .

Justice can't be refused or delayed.

Then in 1492, the Spanish king and queen financed a voyage of discovery by Christopher Columbus.

Columbus arrived at lands unknown to Europeans. It was a "New World" to them, and Europeans meant to have it. Across South and North America, they seized land and its riches, and made colonies for transplanted Europeans at the expense of Native Americans.

In 1608, for example, the French tried to create a North American colony. They killed two Iroquois chiefs, and a long, bitter war followed.

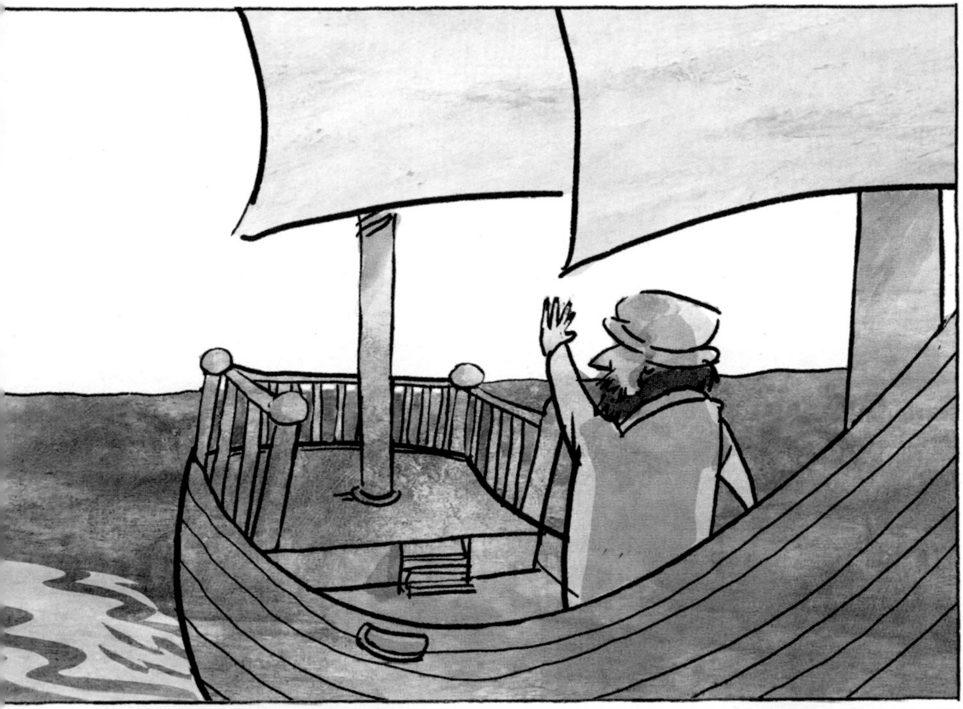

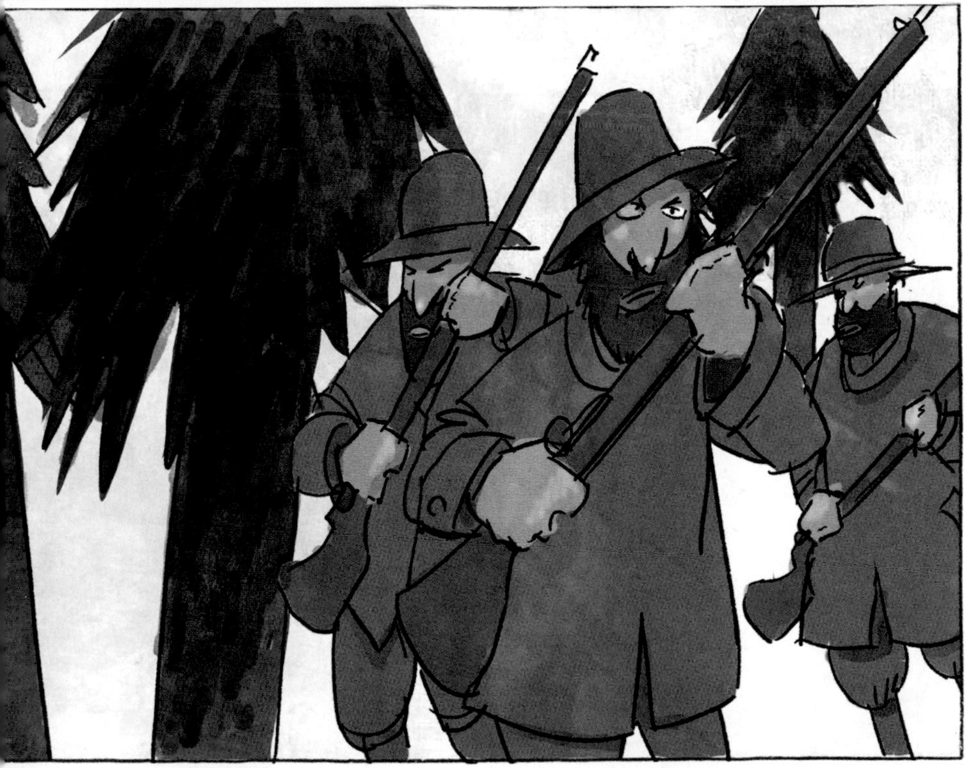

About that same time, England's King James I established two colonies in Virginia.

The one at Roanoke failed and its colonists disappeared . . .

... while the other in Jamestown barely hung on, its people even eating their dead neighbors to escape starvation.

But survive they did.

By July of 1619, Virginia founded the House of Burgesses, a collection of colonists elected by towns and villages to help govern with a king-appointed governor. A burgess is a person from a town or borough. The House of Burgesses was the first democratically elected legislative assembly in the British colonies.

George Washington would eventually serve there for fifteen years, before he went on to bigger things.

We shouldn't be surprised that voting for House of Burgesses' representatives was limited to land-owning . . . men.

A month after the first meeting of the House of Burgesses, and a day's horseback ride away, a ship unloaded about twenty Africans who were sold to colonists. They were just a few of the hundreds of thousands of Africans who would be stolen from their homes and enslaved in North and South America by the Spanish and English. The enslavement of Africans would have enormous consequences for America and its government.

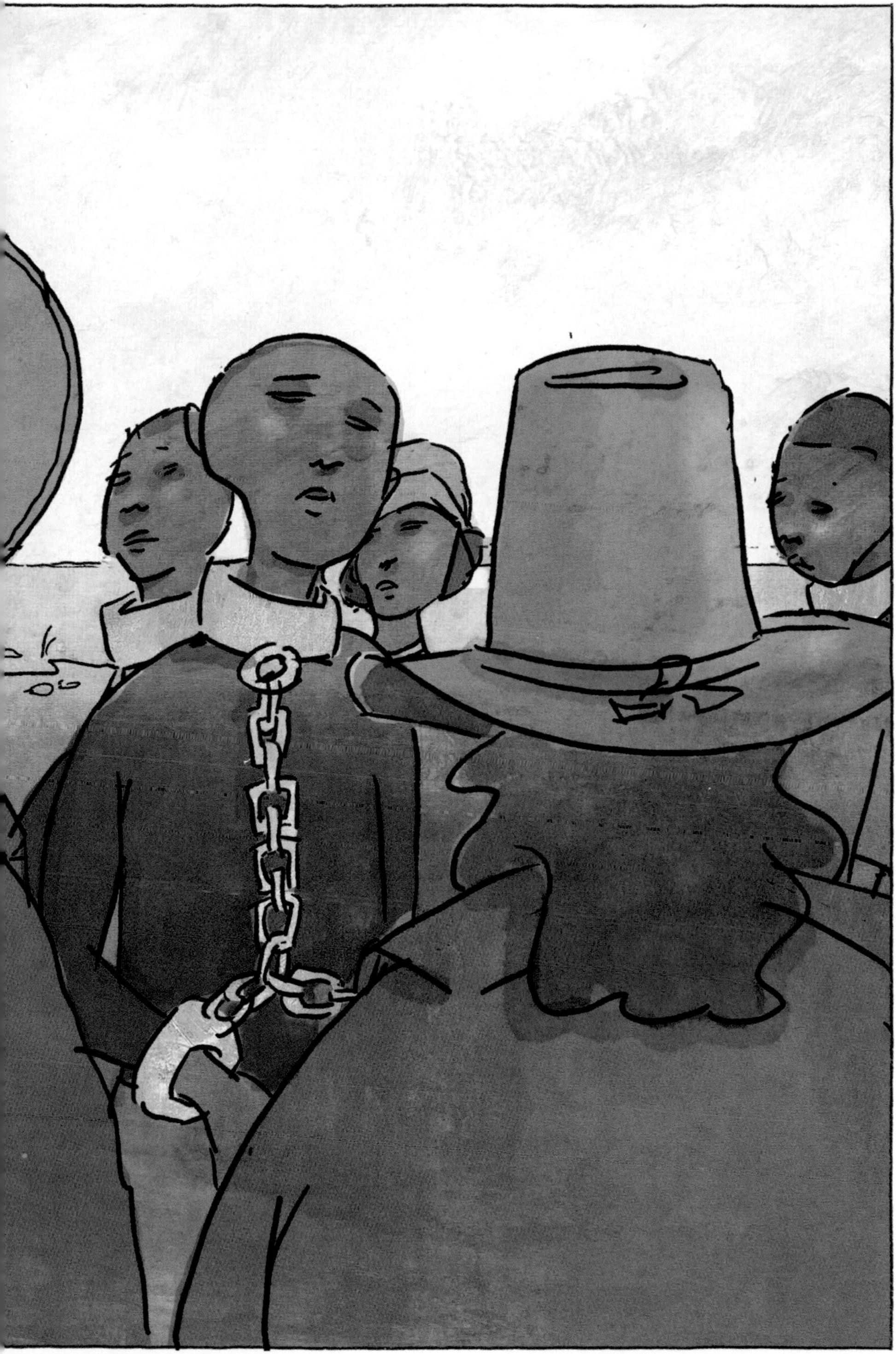

In September 1620, the *Mayflower* sailed the Atlantic, carrying more English colonists bound for Virginia. But they ended up in New England . . . something to do with bad navigation and unforgiving seas, I believe.

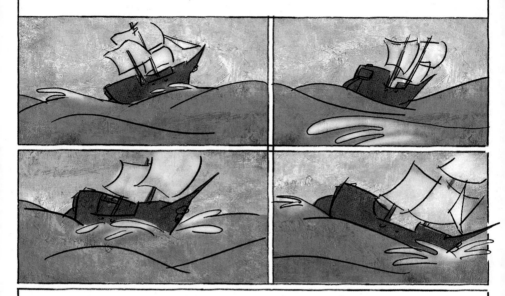

Before leaving their ship, the men set down some rules for their new home, including the agreement to gather now and then in a "Body Politic" where "just and equal Laws" should be enacted for the "general good of the Colony." The agreement was called the Mayflower Compact.

Their concern for justice, however, didn't apply to the Native Peoples whose land they intruded on . . .

The *Mayflower* passengers weren't the only ones thinking about rules and laws and justice. Back in England, around the same time, philosopher John Locke took measure of kings and their powers and found them lacking.

"The state of nature . . . teaches all mankind . . . that being all equal and independent, no one ought to harm another in his life, health, liberty, or possessions . . ."

In other words, a king is no better than anyone else . . .
A very Big Idea for its time.

Locke would live to see England's King Charles I thrown out and replaced by a tyrant, Oliver Cromwell—who ruled like a king—and then see another king—Charles II—installed.
Government could be topsy-turvy!

CHARLES I

OLIVER CROMWELL

CHARLES II

Despite Locke, one-person rule would flourish around the world.

In Japan, shoguns ruled with absolute power. Shogun Tokugawa Ienari held power over a prosperous country for fifty years . . . and fathered fifty-four children along the way.

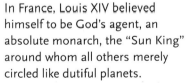

A powerful Catherine the Great—yes, a queen!—expanded Russia's size and power. She also ensured the privilege of Russian nobles while ignoring the plight of slave-like serfs.

In France, Louis XIV believed himself to be God's agent, an absolute monarch, the "Sun King" around whom all others merely circled like dutiful planets.

He rewarded himself with extravagances like the opulent Palace of Versailles and frittered away the royal treasury on wars.

Yes, so many monarchs and one-person rulers! How and when did things change, you ask?

Patience.

In North America, England's colonies grew to thirteen, all acting independently. Colonial leader Ben Franklin believed binding the colonies together would make them stronger.

In 1754, representatives of several colonies met to conclude a treaty with the Haudenosaunee, or Iroquois.

Franklin saw how the Mohawk, Onondaga, Cayuga, Oneida, Seneca, and Tuscarora tribes had joined together for their mutual benefit. He saw how both Iroquois men and women played critical roles in governing. Franklin believed the Iroquois Confederacy was a useful lesson for the colonies.

"It would be a very strange Thing, if six Nations of ignorant Savages should be capable of forming a . . . Union . . . yet . . . a like (similar) Union should be impracticable for ten or a Dozen English Colonies . . ."

"Ignorant savages"? Mr. Franklin should have considered his prejudices.

In any case, the colonists didn't believe they had anything to learn from Native Americans and Franklin's idea went nowhere.

At about that time, England's King George III fought a long and expensive war with the French. With an eye to fatten his shrunken royal treasury, George levied taxes on his thirteen North American colonies, sparking anger, contempt, and defiance from the colonists.

The King ignored the colonists and violence followed.

Boston Massacre

Lexington and Concord

Bunker Hill

On June 7, 1776, the thirteen colonies decided they had had enough. They declared, "these United Colonies are, and of right ought to be, free and independent States . . ."

A republic!

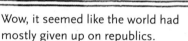

Wow, it seemed like the world had mostly given up on republics.

Five state delegates were appointed to prepare a declaration of independence: My husband, John Adams, and Robert Livingston, Roger Sherman, Ben Franklin, and Thomas Jefferson. Jefferson would write the first draft.

They went to work in a room above a stable.

Most of the document was a collection of complaints against the king, how awful, unfair, and treacherous he was. However, it's not the complaints that we remember, but rather its opening words that put forth ideas that rattled the established world order then . . . and now.

"We hold these truths to be self-evident, that all men are created equal, that they are endowed by their Creator with certain unalienable Rights, that among these are Life, Liberty and the pursuit of Happiness.—That to secure these rights, Governments are instituted among Men, deriving their just powers from the consent of the governed . . ."

Jefferson was saying kings aren't better than anybody else and that the power of government comes from the people being governed.
Astonishing. Big. Idea.

But a Big Idea with a flaw: "Men" meant white landowners and left out everyone else.

Jefferson was—and still is—celebrated for writing those renowned opening words. But he didn't so much write them as *rewrite* them. Several weeks earlier, Virginia politician George Mason had written the Virginia Declaration of Rights . . .

"That all men are by nature equally free and independent and have certain inherent rights . . . namely, the enjoyment of life and liberty, with the means of acquiring and possessing property, and pursuing and obtaining happiness and safety."

Jefferson never denied cribbing Mason's work, explaining that no one was expecting an entirely original declaration. And Mason was also echoing thoughts already voiced by John Locke.

In any case, Jefferson's version is more poetic and memorable. Still, I'm sad George Mason's contribution has been widely forgotten.

The Declaration of Independence was published July 2, 1776, but dated July 4, 1776.

"The colonists greeted it with cheers, bells, and cannons. The American Revolution was *on*!"

The actual Declaration of Independence went in and out of storage, was treated with little care, and was allowed to fade until it was given a proper and permanent home in 1924. But its ideas never lost their strength. It would be a "standard against which to measure the nation again and again."

It was that standard that an African American freeman named Prince Hall used when he petitioned the Massachusetts legislature to emancipate enslaved people in the state. Six months after the Declaration was announced, he wrote that enslaved people . . .

". . . have in Common with all other men a Natural and unalienable Right to that freedom which the Great Parent of the Universe hath Bestowed equally on all Mankind."

Hall's petition was a start; slavery ended in Massachusetts in 1783.

But despite Hall, slavery was widely practiced by many, including—let's not forget—some of the signers of the Declaration of Independence.

JOHN HANCOCK

GEORGE CLINTON

William FLOYD

THOMAS JEFFERSON

GEORGE REED

RoBERT LIVINGSTON

RiCHARD HENRY LEE

BEN FRANKLIN

RoBERT MORRIS

English armies lost to those of the thirteen colonies led by George Washington. His astonishing victory was matched by his actions afterward. Instead of using the deeply felt loyalty of his troops and his widespread popularity to seize power, as many other great generals had done across history, Washington stepped down and accepted democratic, civilian rule. I don't know if you can call it a Big Idea, but it was a Big and Influential Gesture.

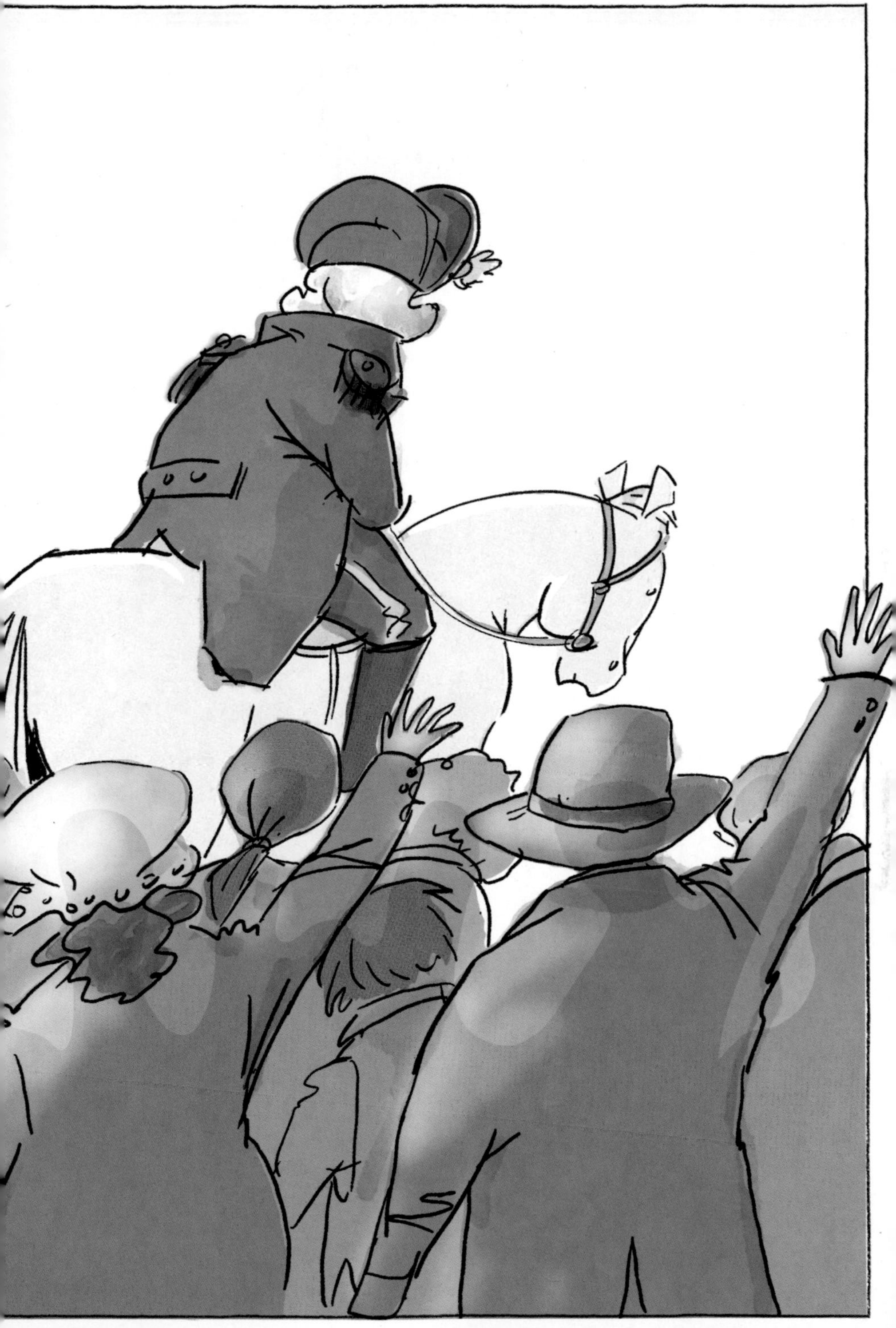

The Articles were less a great bear hug of former colonies and more a feeble grasping of fingertips.

The Confederation couldn't easily raise money,

and it couldn't regulate trade between the states.

It had no premier, prime minister, or president. It lacked courts.

It was an unhappy mess.

"Thirteen Sovereignties pulling against each other . . . will soon bring ruin on the whole."

Perhaps greater attention should have been paid to the Iroquois Confederacy!

MADISON

Virginia politician James Madison saw the Articles' failings and cast around for a remedy. With help from Alexander Hamilton, Madison convinced the government to call an assembly at Philadelphia of specially selected state delegates "for the sole and express purpose of revising the Articles of Confederation."

In 1787, four years after the end of the Revolutionary War, seventy-five delegates were selected from twelve states; Rhode Island sent none. But only fifty-five attended. Many would come and go to attend to other business, so for much of the time, only about thirty delegates were present for discussion and debate. Most were well educated. Some were lawyers. Some had served as military officers in the Revolution.

And, yes . . . all were white men.

A few delegates arrived early, including Madison, George Washington, and Ben Franklin. They gathered at Franklin's home and agreed to ignore the instruction to revise the existing Articles and concoct a brand-new constitution instead.

A constitution is a document that sets down the powers and duties of government.

It wasn't anything new; constitutions had been around for centuries. One, the Manden Charter, was adopted by West Africans in the thirteenth century. It addressed diversity, the sacredness of the human being, education, food security, the abolition of slavery by raid, and freedom of expression and trade.

James Madison, small and frail, would prove to be an outsized contributor to the creation and adoption of the Constitution.

He envisioned a government of three parts, or branches, whose power came from the people.

"Let Congress legislate, let others execute, let others judge."

LEGISLATORS

EXECUTIVE

JUDGES

That is, one branch would make laws, another would carry them out, and the third would decide when laws were broken.

If you think this all sounds like the ancient Greek and Roman republics, you'd be right. Madison, Hamilton, Franklin, Washington, and the rest were spellbound by everything Greek and Roman.

The three-branch-government scheme would be known as the Virginia Plan, taking its name from its Virginian sponsors.

The Constitutional Convention began on May 25, 1787. The delegates gathered in the same room in which the Declaration of Independence had been debated and signed.

The distracting clip-clop of passing horse-drawn wagons was dampened by dirt thrown over roadway cobblestones.

The windows were nailed shut, trapping in the stuffy summer air,

but also shutting in the delegates' discussions while shutting out nosey eavesdroppers . . .

and the swarming flies of summer.

Sentries were posted at the doors, too. The delegates agreed to keep their conversations secret in the hope of free discussions without public second-guessing.

Washington was elected convention presiding officer, or president.

Edmund Randolph of Virginia, an ally of James Madison, offered the Virginia Plan to the delegates.

VIRGINIA PLAN

They decided each state would have an equal vote on proposals.

The idea of replacing the Articles entirely with a *national* government didn't go over well with everyone. William Paterson of New Jersey pressed for a stronger, improved Articles of Confederation, but the Articles nevertheless.

NEW JERSEY PLAN

The so-called New Jersey Plan was voted down.

Alexander Hamilton of New York had a Big Idea. Believing people "were tired of the excesses of democracy," he suggested a government where the legislature made all the laws, states would be led by appointed governors, and the senators would serve for life, as would the chief executive who would also have the power to cancel any laws.

Hmmm . . . that seems very much like the king and monarchy the Revolution had just cast off.
The convention delegates thought so, too, and Hamilton's Big Idea went nowhere.

The Virginia Plan still held the greatest promise. Debates now centered on its details.
There was a lot of talk about the two-part legislature. The Virginia Plan's scheme included one legislative part with elected members. The other part would be drawn from members of the first. Representation would be proportioned by population—that is, the states with more people would have more representatives than those with fewer.

It's not surprising the smaller states cringed at the idea, fearing their influence would be overrun by the larger states.

And Southern states wanted their enslaved people to be counted as residents, increasing the South's representation and power.

Northerners thought it nonsense.

Slavery opponent Elbridge Gerry of Massachusetts asked acidly, "Why, then, should the blacks, who were property in the South, be in the rule of representation more than the cattle and horses of the North?"

And if enslaved people were counted for representation, Northerners continued, then they should be subject to apportioned taxes, too.

Higher taxes? The Southerners wouldn't have any of that.

The logjam threatened the entire convention with collapse.

The standstill was broken by Connecticut's Roger Sherman and Oliver Ellsworth.

ROGER SHERMAN   OLIVER ELLSWORTH

HOUSE of REPRESENTATIVES   SENATE

Their Connecticut, or Great, Compromise called for a House of Representatives that would be proportioned by population and a Senate in which each state had an equal vote.

For purposes of representation and taxation, all of a state's white, free people would be counted, and "all other persons" counted as three-fifths of a free person.

"All other persons" meant enslaved Black people. Nowhere in the Constitution will you find the words *slavery*, *enslavement*, or *enslaved person*.

Were they ashamed to admit it existed?

Native Americans were mentioned in the Great Compromise, too. They would not be counted toward representation because they were not citizens. If they left tribal lands and paid taxes, then they'd be counted . . . but they still couldn't vote.

The convention delegates hammered out more details.

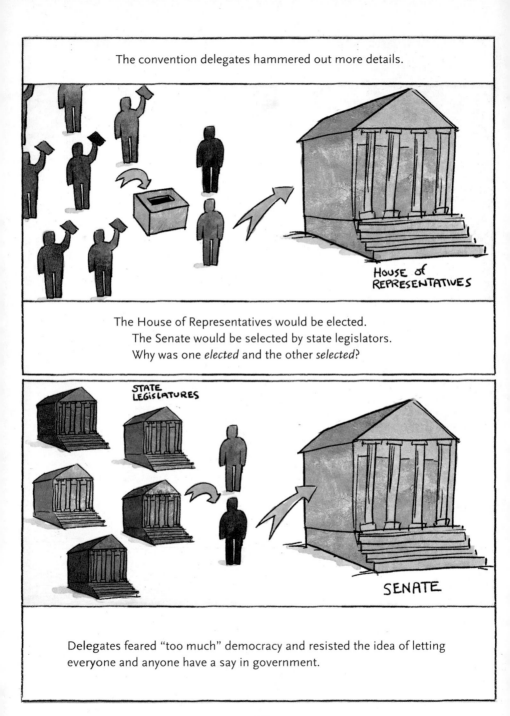

The House of Representatives would be elected.
The Senate would be selected by state legislators.
Why was one *elected* and the other *selected*?

Delegates feared "too much" democracy and resisted the idea of letting everyone and anyone have a say in government.

They were suspicious of people who had "little property, education, or principle."

Better to leave governing to a *special* few.

It was an opinion they applied to the selection of a president. Instead of being elected by citizens, state legislators would appoint electors who would then choose the president.

ELECTORS

PRESIDENT

After four months of arguing, discussing, bickering, and debating, they were done. It was left to Gouverneur Morris of New York to take all the decisions and compromises and write them in clear and precise language.

It begins . . .

"We, the People of the United States, in Order to form a more perfect Union, establish Justice, insure domestic Tranquility, provide for the common defence, promote the general Welfare, and secure the Blessings of Liberty to ourselves and our Posterity, do ordain and establish this Constitution for the United States of America."

A Perfect Union? I like the sound of that Big Idea.
    The preamble, or opening, is both a promise and a challenge to the new republic.

After the final draft was approved, it was given to clerk Jacob Shallus to make a neat version for signing. Forty hours later, he was done.

On September 17, 1787, thirty-nine delegates signed. Three delegates refused. Copies were made of the Constitution and carried away on horse-drawn stagecoaches. Soon it was reprinted everywhere. And everywhere the question arose:

Are you for or against it?

Oh, there were many against it, and complaints were numerous.

The Constitution gave the national government too much power and the states too little, opponents said. It delivered power to a small group of powerful and wealthy people.

"These lawyers, and men of learning, and moneyed men . . . expect to be the managers of this Constitution, and get all the power . . . and then they will swallow up all us little folks . . . just as the whale swallowed up Jonah. This is what I am afraid of . . ."

You're mistaken,

replied the supporters of the new government. Built into the Constitution are checks and balances to limit the national government's power. And besides, with the new Constitution . . .

". . . excellences of republican government may be retained and its imperfections lessened or avoided,"

that is, the Constitution will let us have the good parts of government and less of the bad stuff. And besides, failing to approve the Constitution meant remaining with the feeble and failing Articles of Confederation.

Argument for and against bred mayhem. Copies of the Constitution were burned in public by its opponents. Fist fights and rioting erupted.

"A disturbance in Albany, New York . . . occasioned bloodshed."

Nine of the thirteen colonies needed to ratify, or accept, the Constitution for it to become the law of the land. Conventions of specially selected delegates were assembled in each state to decide, except for Rhode Island, which allowed its citizens a direct vote on its passage.

By January 1788, Pennsylvania, New Jersey, Delaware, Georgia, and Connecticut had ratified. Then Massachusetts approved, but only after it was assured the Constitution would be slightly amended, or changed, to include a list of rights, like freedom of speech and religion. Maryland and South Carolina followed.

Rhode Island voters rejected the Constitution by a margin of ten to one.

But on June 21, 1788, New Hampshire became the ninth state to ratify . . .
The Constitution had passed and America was on its way to a Perfect Union!

New York City celebrated with a great parade of marchers, horse-drawn floats, and bands.

And Rhode Island? It eventually agreed to join the new states in 1790.

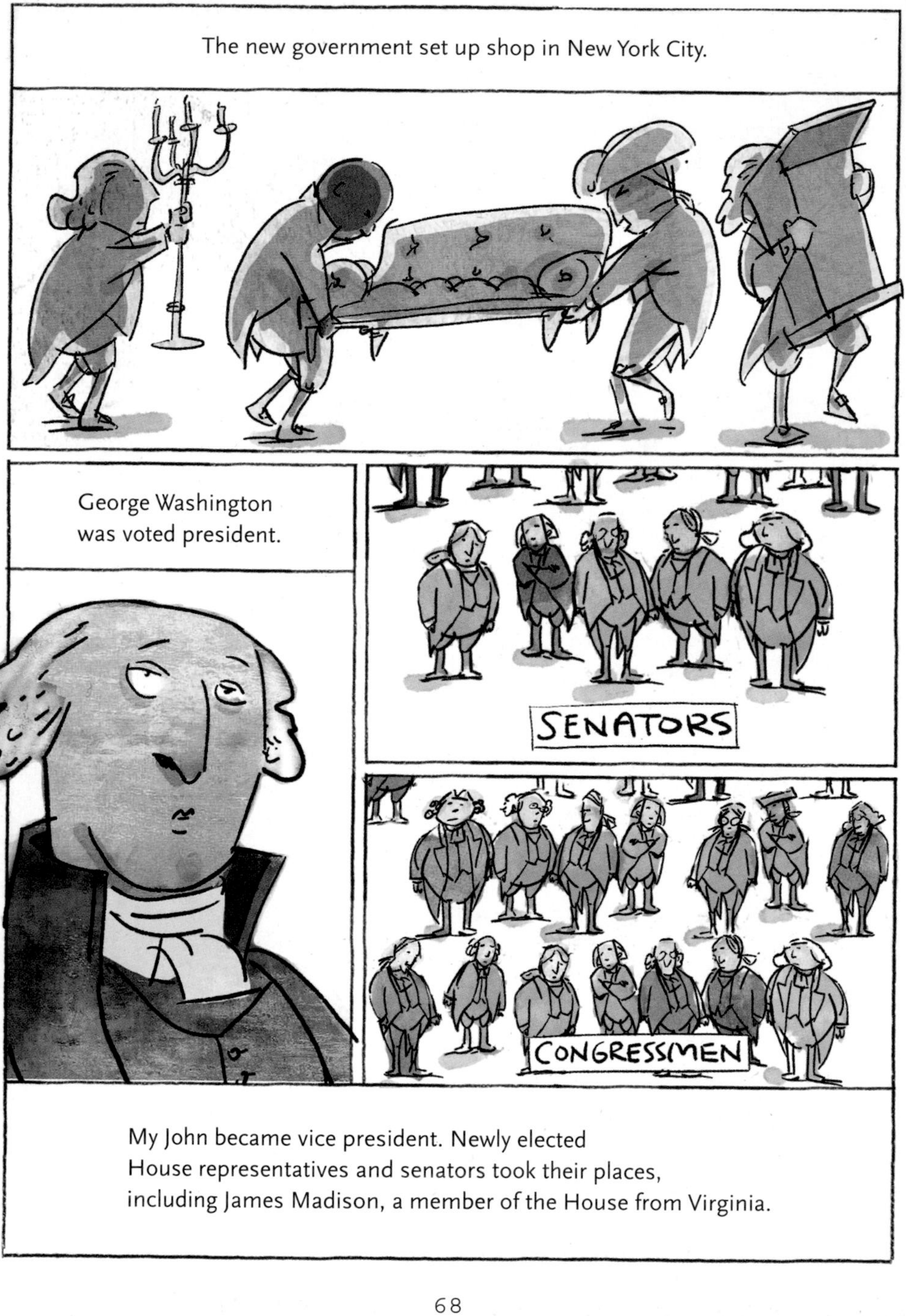
The new government set up shop in New York City.
George Washington was voted president.
SENATORS
CONGRESSMEN
My John became vice president. Newly elected House representatives and senators took their places, including James Madison, a member of the House from Virginia.

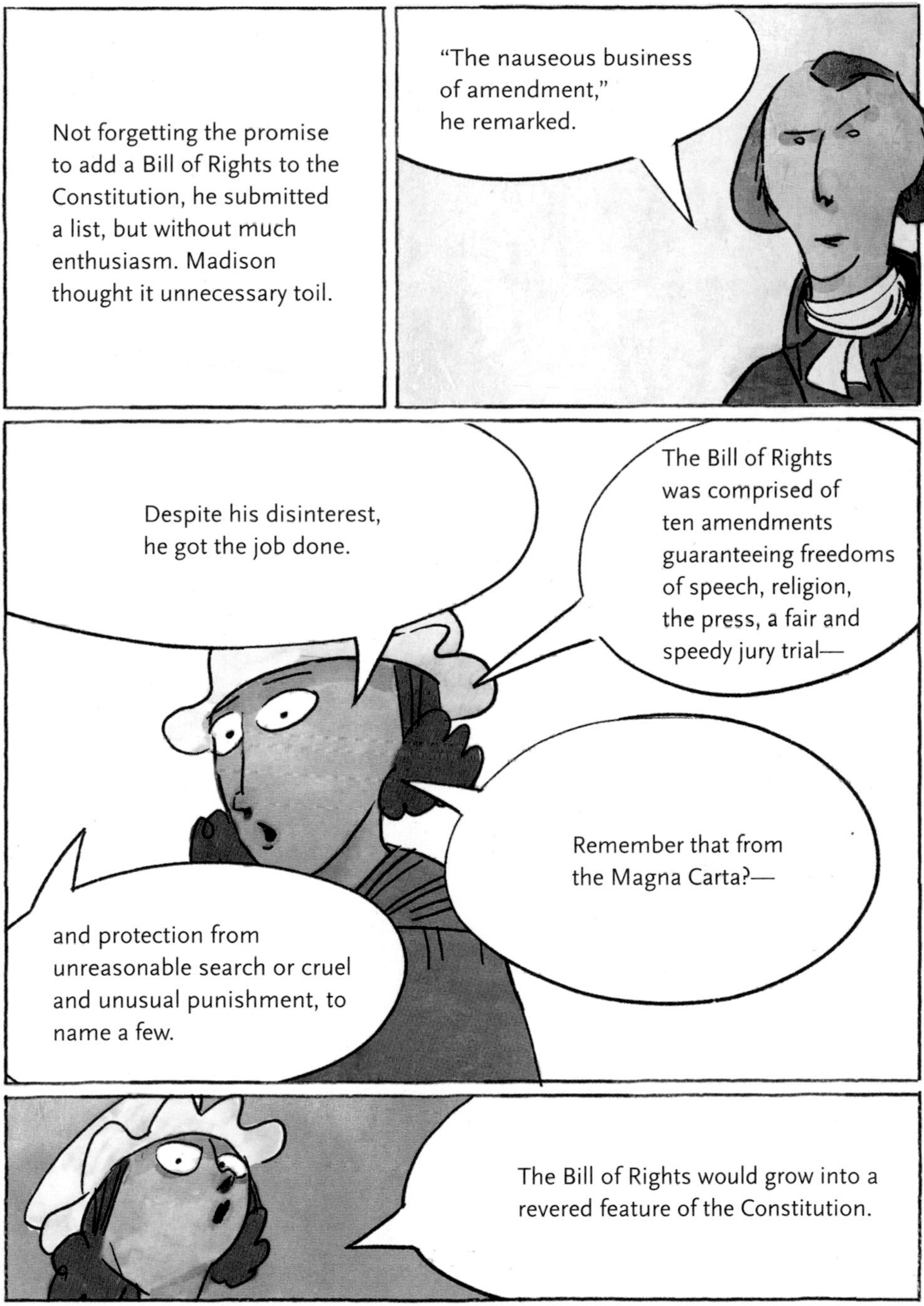
Not forgetting the promise to add a Bill of Rights to the Constitution, he submitted a list, but without much enthusiasm. Madison thought it unnecessary toil.
"The nauseous business of amendment," he remarked.
Despite his disinterest, he got the job done.
The Bill of Rights was comprised of ten amendments guaranteeing freedoms of speech, religion, the press, a fair and speedy jury trial—
Remember that from the Magna Carta?—
and protection from unreasonable search or cruel and unusual punishment, to name a few.
The Bill of Rights would grow into a revered feature of the Constitution.

But even with the Bill of Rights, a Perfect Union the United States was not.

A shadow hung over it . . . slavery.

I thought it a sin and believed enslaved people had "as good a right to freedom as we have."

It was abolished in the North but flourished in the South. As America grew west—

mostly at the expense of the Native Americans living there, I might add—and new states joined the original thirteen, people began to argue, bicker, seethe over the expansion of slavery.

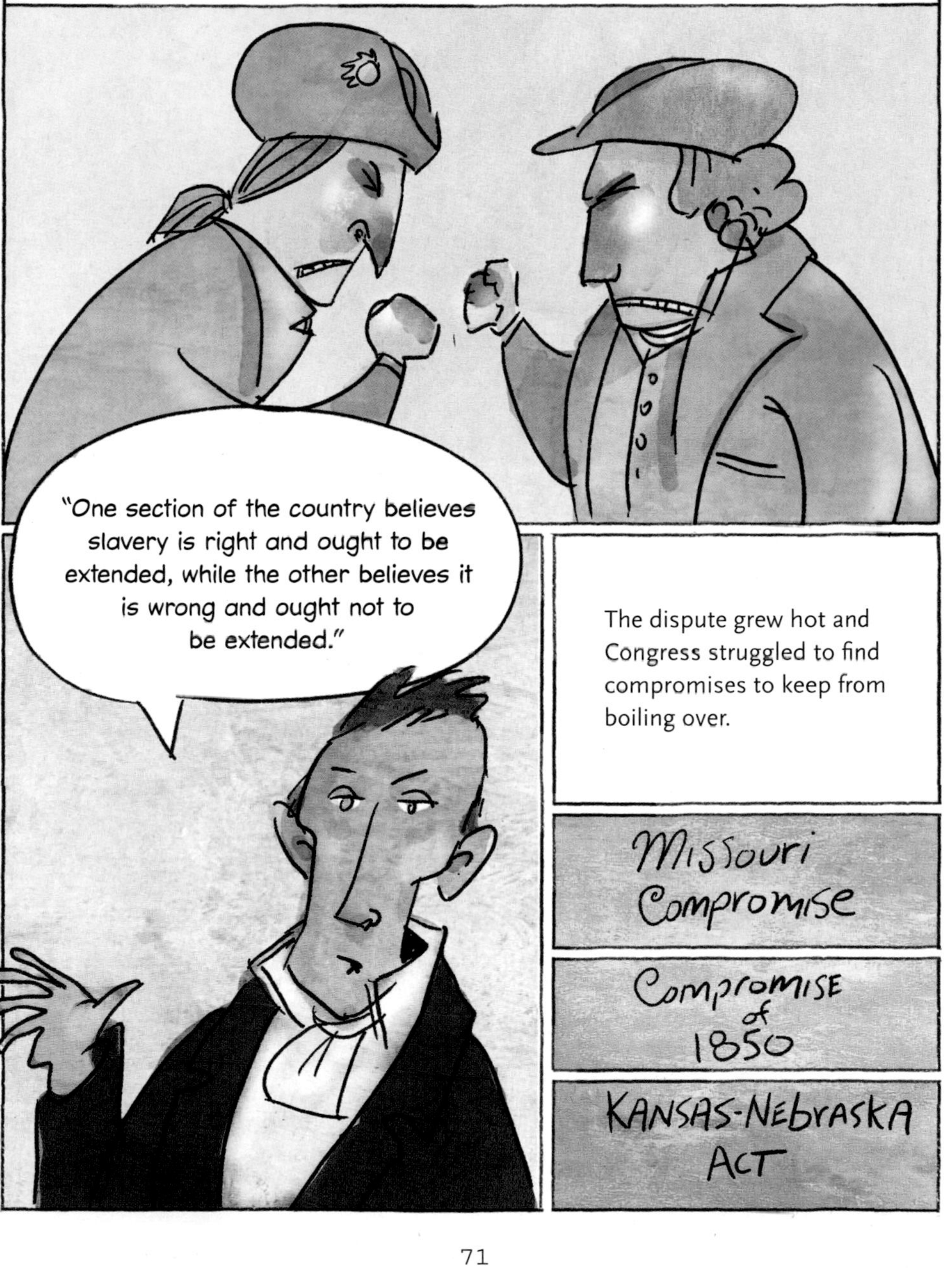
"One section of the country believes slavery is right and ought to be extended, while the other believes it is wrong and ought not to be extended."
The dispute grew hot and Congress struggled to find compromises to keep from boiling over.
Missouri Compromise
Compromise of 1850
KANSAS-NEBRASKA ACT

Then in 1857, the United States Supreme Court ruled that an enslaved man, Dred Scott, could not be granted freedom simply by having lived for a time in a free state.

SLAVE STATE

FREE STATE

SLAVE STATE

Chief Justice Roger B. Taney explained Black people were not citizens.

He said the Constitution gave Black people ". . . no rights which the white man was bound to respect; and that the negro might justly and lawfully be reduced to slavery for his benefit. [Black people could be] bought and sold and treated as an ordinary article of merchandise . . ."

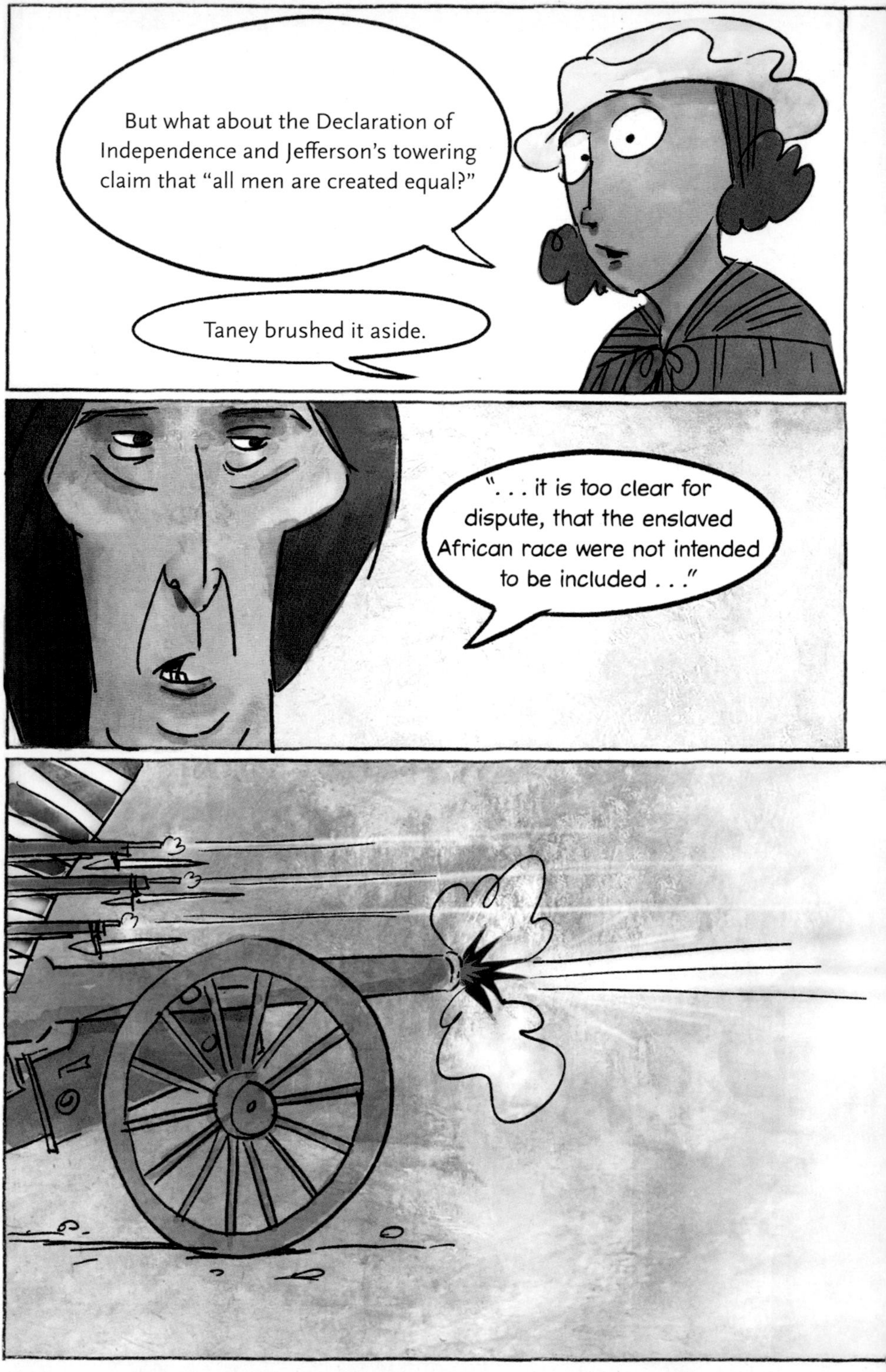
But what about the Declaration of Independence and Jefferson's towering claim that "all men are created equal?"
Taney brushed it aside.
". . . it is too clear for dispute, that the enslaved African race were not intended to be included . . ."

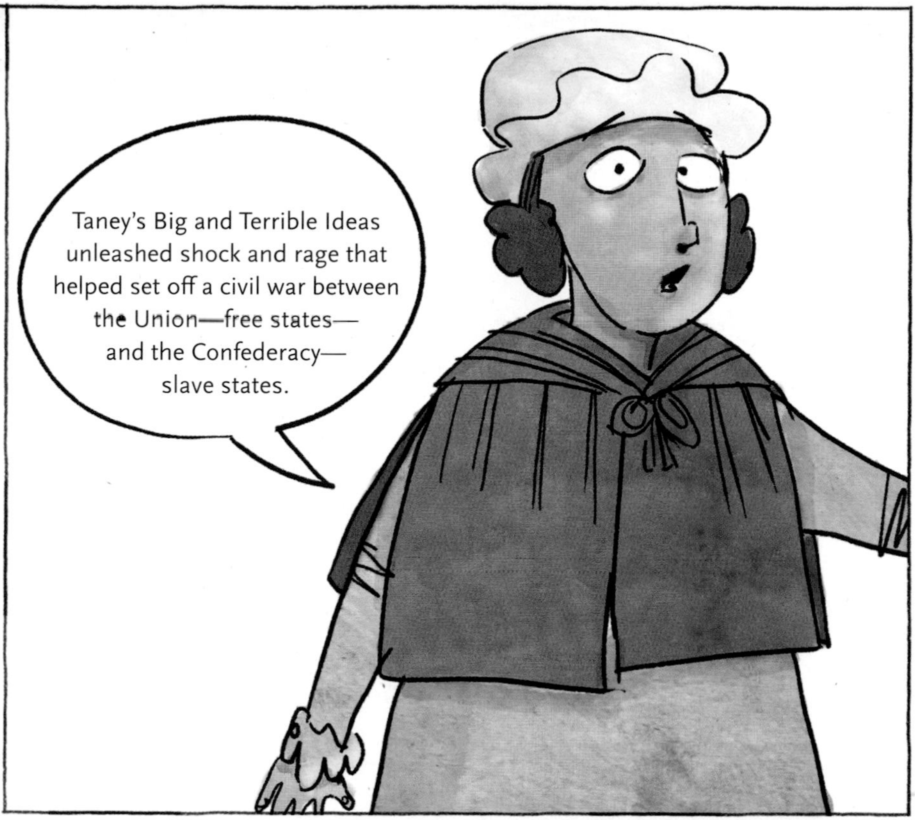
Taney's Big and Terrible Ideas unleashed shock and rage that helped set off a civil war between the Union—free states— and the Confederacy— slave states.

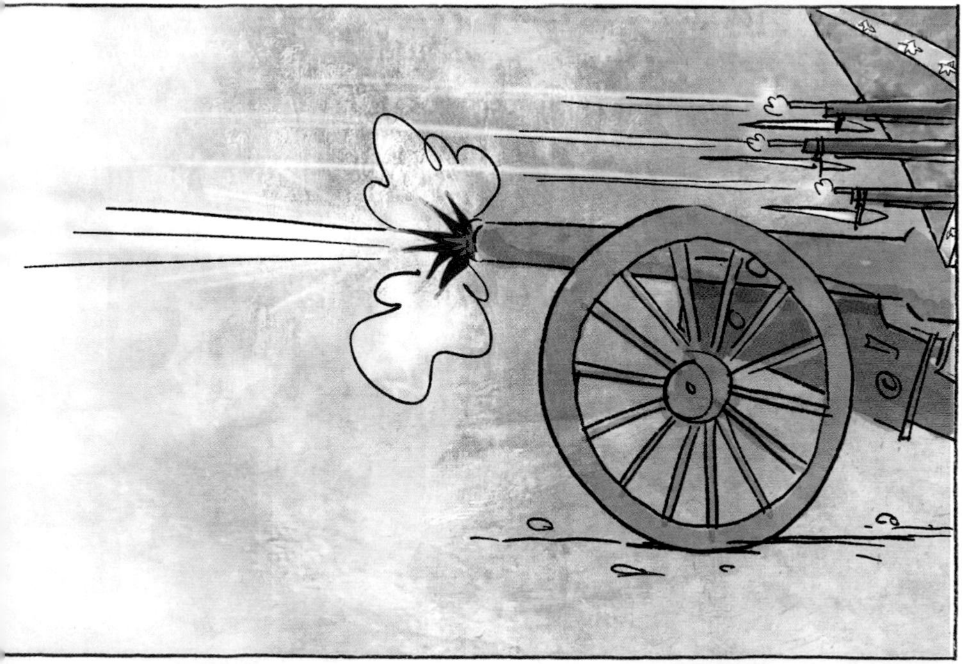

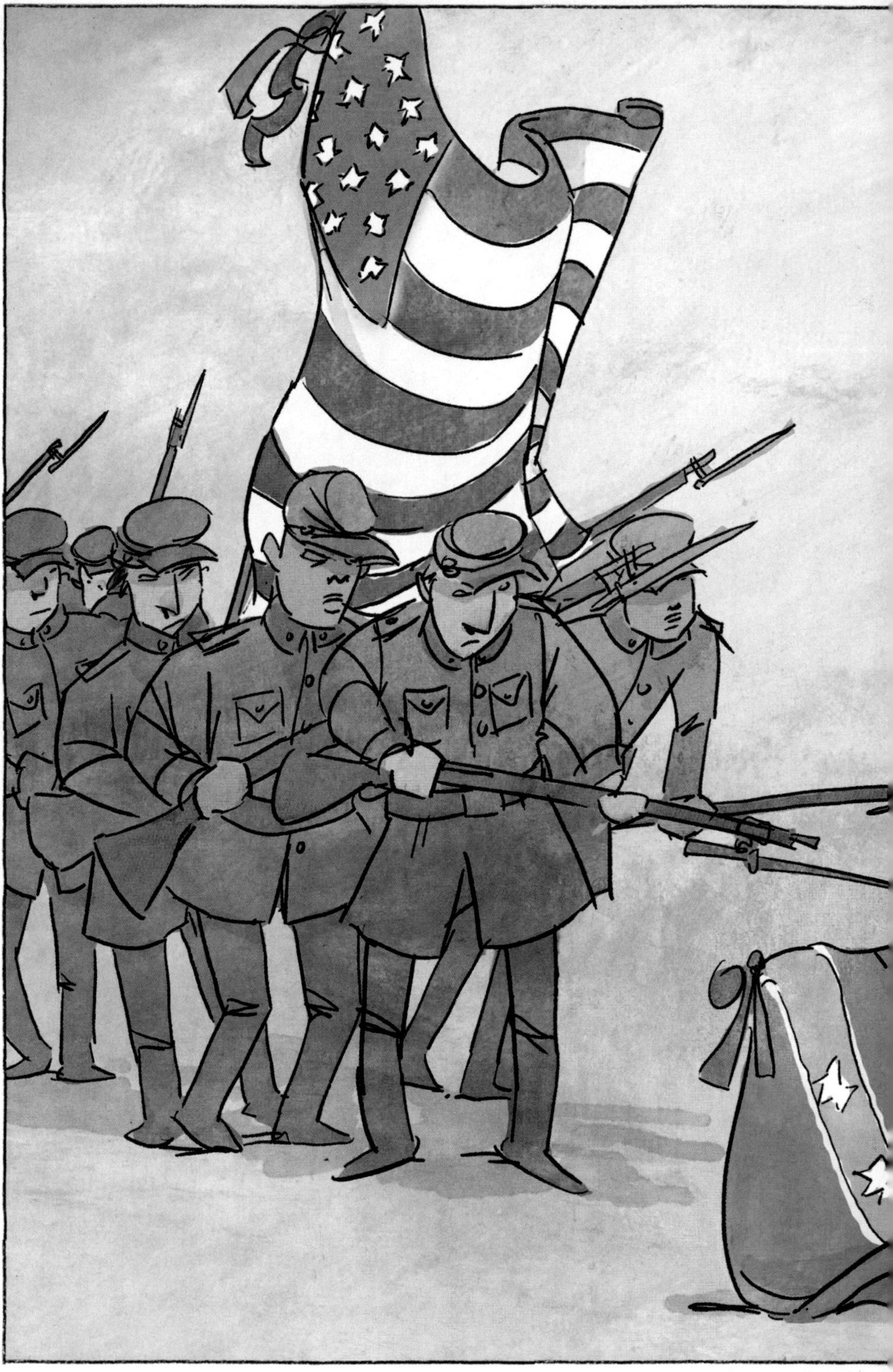

After five years and hundreds of thousands of casualties, the Union prevailed.

America bound up its wounds and added three amendments to the U.S. Constitution.

CONSTITUTION

We the People...

The Thirteenth Amendment ended slavery in America.

13TH

14TH

15TH

The Fourteenth Amendment declared that a person's life, liberty, or property couldn't be taken away without due process of law, and that everyone was guaranteed equal protection of the law. And no longer would a Black person be counted as three-fifths of a white one in regard to representation; African Americans would be counted as whole people.

The Fifteenth Amendment stated that the right to vote should not be denied or curtailed because of race, color, or previous condition of servitude.

For several years after the war, the Union oversaw the former Confederate states. During this time of "Reconstruction," African Americans were elected to a variety of positions.

As one freedman who became an Alabama legislator explained,

"I walked out (of slavery) like a man and shouldered my responsibilities."

In 1870, formerly enslaved Hiram Revels became the first African American U.S. senator.

He was followed in 1875 by Blanche K. Bruce.

But the Big Idea of a Perfect Union that embraced former enslaved people vanished when Reconstruction ended. The Union's oversight of the South ended. Terrorist groups like the Ku Klux Klan attacked and murdered Black people who tried to vote or hold office.

Legislatures across the old Confederacy passed laws that undercut Black people's right to vote.

". . . we hold this to be a Government of White People, made and to be perpetuated for the exclusive benefit of the White race, and . . . that the people of African descent cannot be considered as citizens of the United States."

Reading tests were applied to Black voters, most of whom had little to no schooling.

They were required to pay a tax to vote.

They encountered confusing and complicated voting registration schemes.

Didn't the laws hurt poor and uneducated whites, too? Powerful elites didn't seem to care so long as they could hold on to power.

Other laws limited African Americans' job prospects, undermined their education, and degraded their culture.

The anti-Black laws were commonly known as "Jim Crow," taken from a kind of theater performance in which a white man would blacken his face and portray a Black man in a degrading and insulting manner.

Black people, it became apparent, were not included in the "We the people" of the Constitution.
And, women were excluded, too.

Women were denied education and some jobs simply because they were women.

Married women were denied the right to own property,

to sign contracts,

to control their own finances.

And women couldn't vote.
In 1848, at Seneca Falls, New York, women held a convention to protest their limited prospects.
Modifying the Declaration of Independence, the Seneca Falls Convention declared . . .

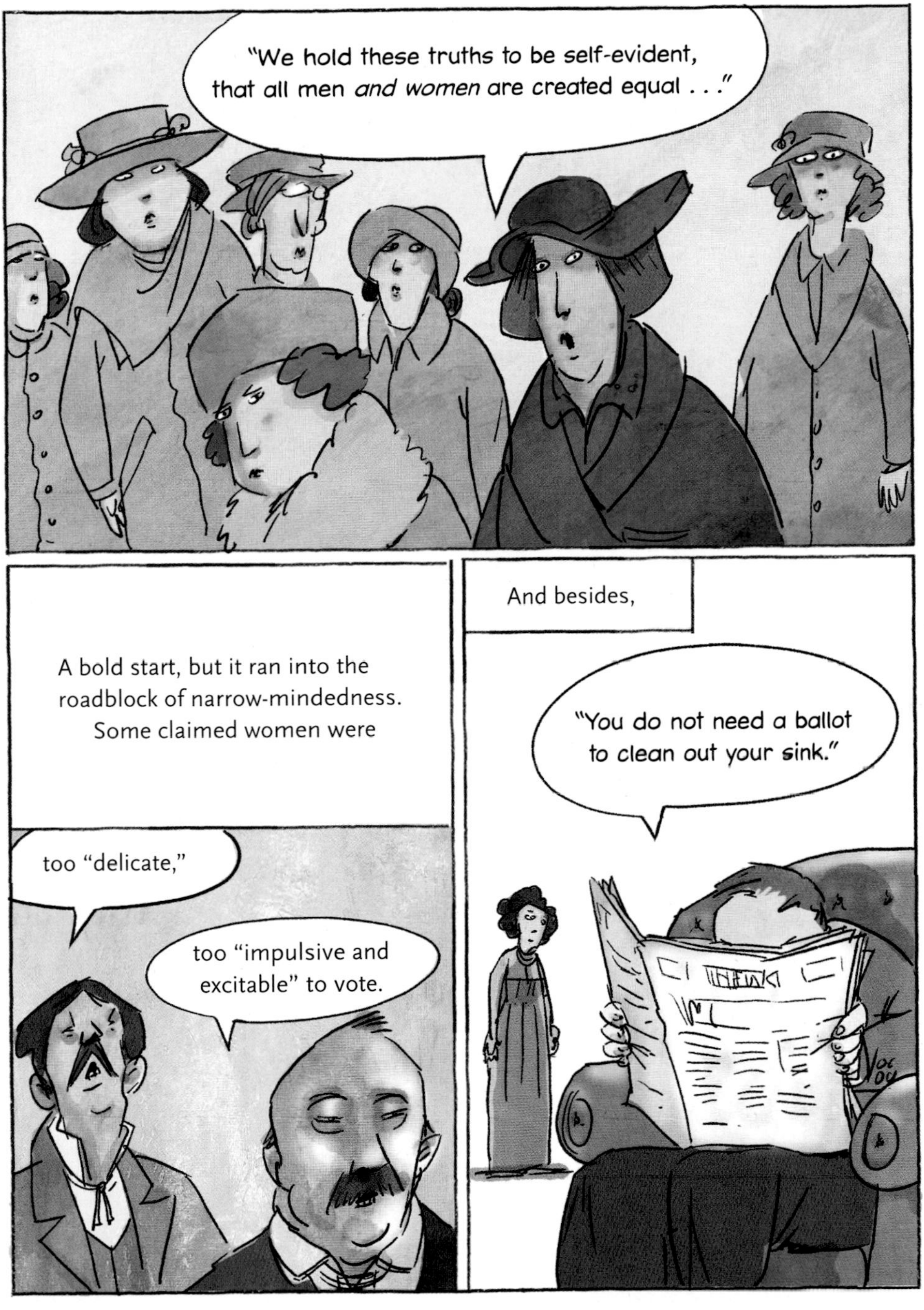
"We hold these truths to be self-evident, that all men *and women* are created equal . . ."
A bold start, but it ran into the roadblock of narrow-mindedness. Some claimed women were
too "delicate,"
too "impulsive and excitable" to vote.
And besides,
"You do not need a ballot to clean out your sink."

The old prejudices proved hard to shake, and twenty-five years after the Seneca Convention, women were still without the right to vote. Nevertheless, hundreds of women cast ballots anyway during the 1872 presidential election. Or tried to. Some were turned away. Others were arrested.

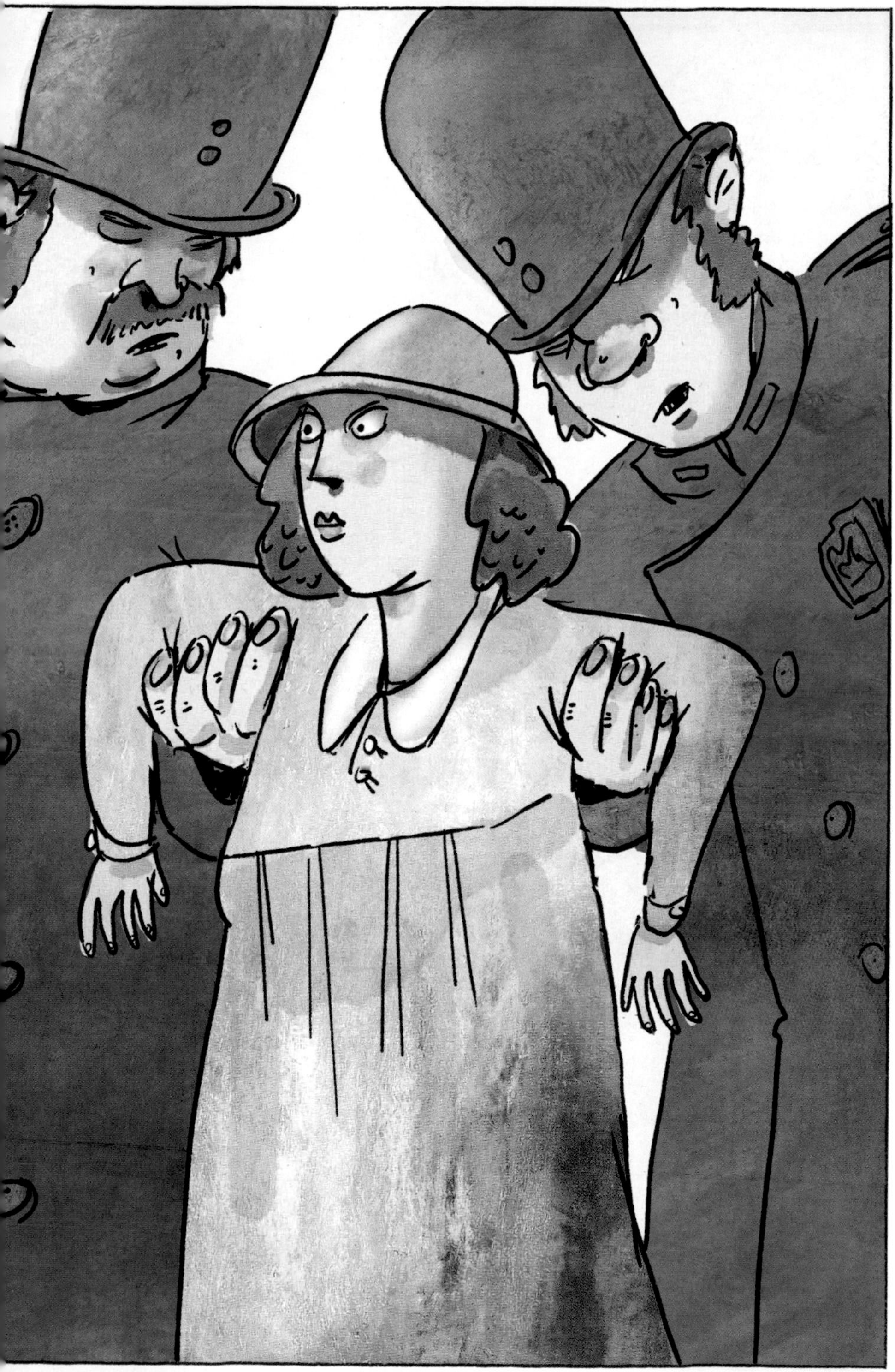

In Missouri, Virginia Minor attempted to register to vote and was snubbed. She protested, arguing that if citizen-men could vote, then citizen-women should be able to vote, too.

She pointed to the Fourteenth Amendment and its guarantee of "equal protection."

Her lawsuit made it all the way to the Supreme Court.

The unanimous court, led by Chief Justice Waite, decided in 1874 that Minor couldn't vote because the

Constitution of the United States does "not necessarily confer the right of suffrage [that is, the right to vote]" upon anyone.

Oh my.

The court made the argument that citizenship came with certain privileges *but voting wasn't one of them.*

My, my.

The legislatures of Southern states seized on the decision to limit Black people's right to vote, too.

In another decision in 1896, the court said that it was legal to have separate railroad cars, bus seats, hospitals, hotels, playgrounds, and schools for Black people as long as they were "equal" to those for white people.

Time would prove that facilities might be separate, but they were never equal.

The separation of Black and white people—segregation—became the new normal. Black people could not . . .

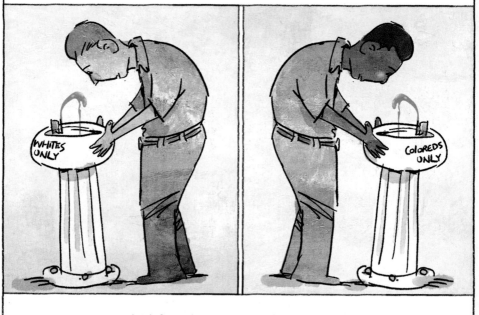

drink from the same water fountain as . . .

share a lunch counter with . . .

or play baseball alongside of a white person.

Checkers players in Birmingham, Alabama, could end up in jail if one was white and the other Black.

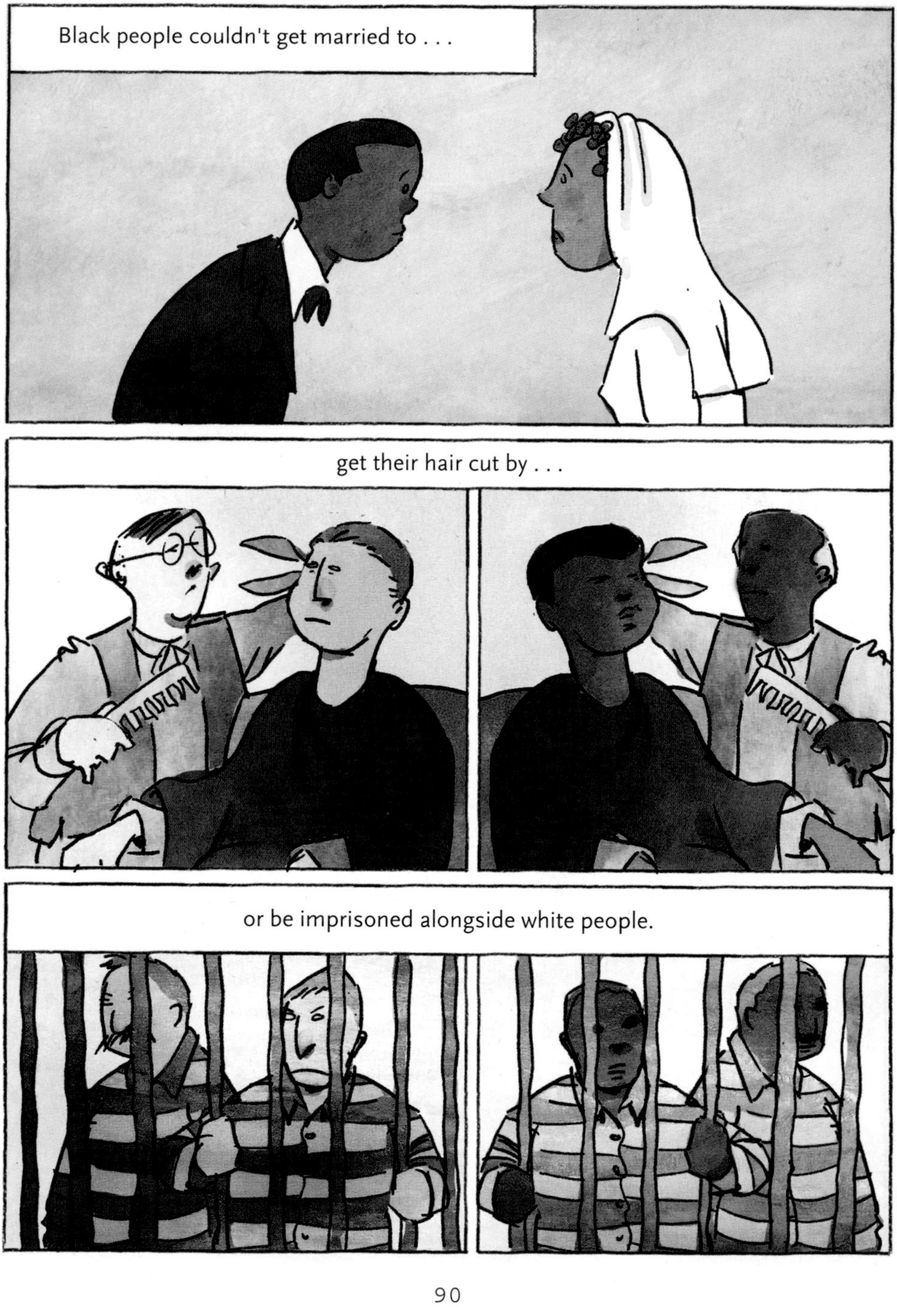
Black people couldn't get married to . . .
get their hair cut by . . .
or be imprisoned alongside white people.

Even the ABCs were segregated; Black and white kids could not go to school together.

Discrimination didn't end with African Americans. Congress passed the Chinese Exclusion Act in 1882. It stopped Chinese immigrants from coming to the United States. And the Chinese already in the country? They were prohibited from becoming citizens.

Still, here and there, were victories for a Perfect Union.

In 1913, the Seventeenth Amendment to the Constitution let voters have a direct say in the election of senators, stripping state legislatures of that power.

In the meanwhile, women paraded and marched for their rights, suffering arrest along the way, perhaps stirred by my pledge in 1776 that . . .

"(Women) . . . will not hold ourselves bound by any laws in which we have no voice or representation."

The push for women's suffrage made headway. Starting in 1890, individual states allowed women to vote, until there were more than two dozen.

WYOMING
COLORADO
UTAH
IDAHO
WASHINGTON
CALIFORNIA
ARIZONA
KANSAS
OREGON
MONTANA
NEVADA
NEW YORK
MICHIGAN
OKLAHOMA
SOUTH DAKOTA

Finally in 1920, the Nineteenth Amendment gave women the right to vote.

But the victory was mostly reserved for white women. Black women, along with Black men, were still afflicted by antidemocratic Jim Crow laws and beset by violence.

Native Americans faced the same stumbling blocks as Black people: poll taxes, literacy tests, and intimidation. Then a 1924 federal law gave them the right to vote. Despite the law, states dragged their feet, and about forty years passed before Native Americans could vote in every state.

The 1940s brought the turmoil of World War II. Making battleships, bombers, bullets, and such required workers, and women stepped in to fill the jobs left by men leaving for the army and navy. Black people found work, too, though President Roosevelt first had to issue an order to ban discrimination in hiring.

Good for the president, but he kept the military segregated;
Black and white people fought separately.

And he had more than a hundred thousand Japanese Americans imprisoned
because of the belief that their loyalty lay not with the United States but with
Japan, America's foe in the war. Italy and Germany were our enemies, too, but
there weren't wholesale roundups of Italian Americans and German Americans.

After the war, African Americans kept pressing for their civil rights. In Topeka, Kansas, Black parents argued that segregated schools were unfair and did not provide "equal justice" as guaranteed by the Constitution.

The dispute was known as *Brown v. Board of Education*—Oliver Brown was one of the people who had filed suit against the Topeka school system—and it ended up in the Supreme Court.

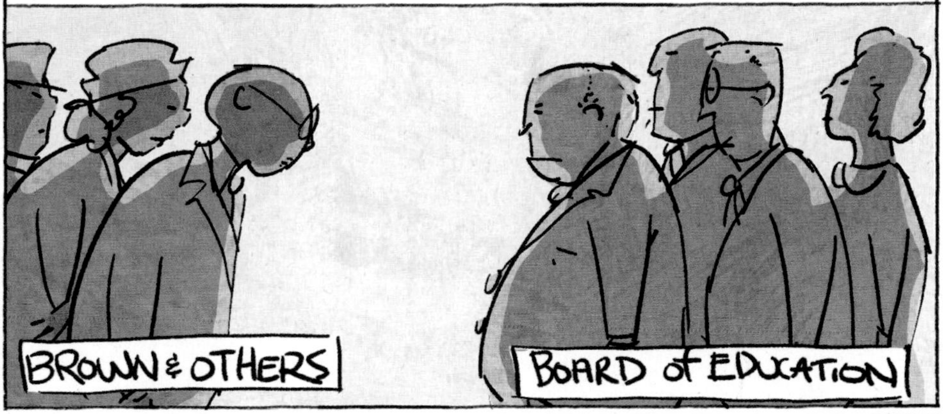
BROWN & OTHERS
BOARD OF EDUCATION

In 1954, the Supreme Court ruled against the school board. Chief Justice Earl Warren wrote . . .

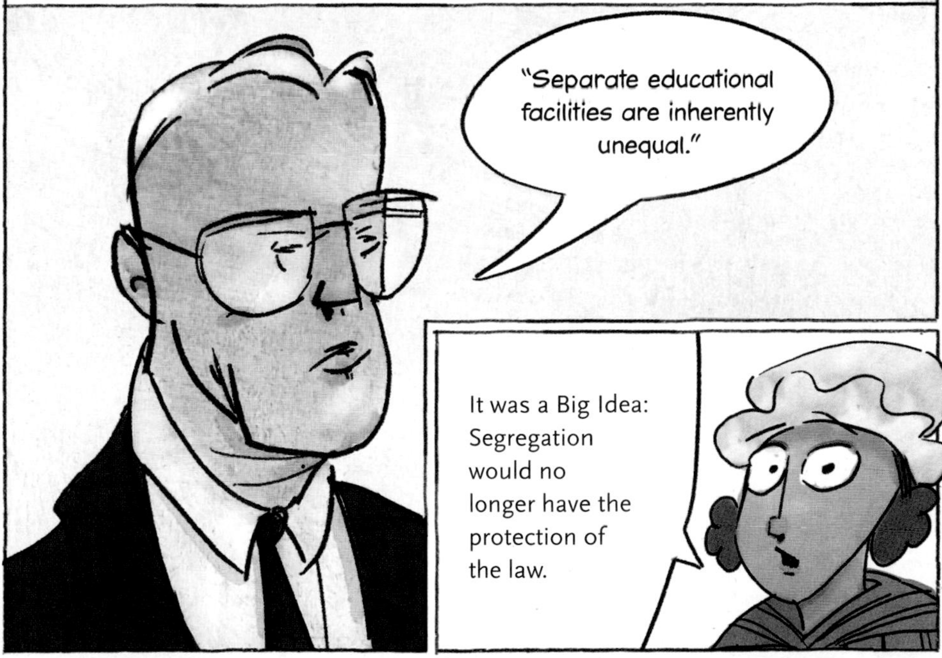
"Separate educational facilities are inherently unequal."
It was a Big Idea: Segregation would no longer have the protection of the law.

Despite the court's decision, many schools refused to desegregate. The governor of Arkansas blocked the admission of nine Black students into an all-white Little Rock high school.

Army troops were sent to ensure the students were granted entrance. The governor backed down but the Little Rock Nine would be insulted and bullied throughout the school term.

It wouldn't be the only time federal forces would be needed to desegregate a school.

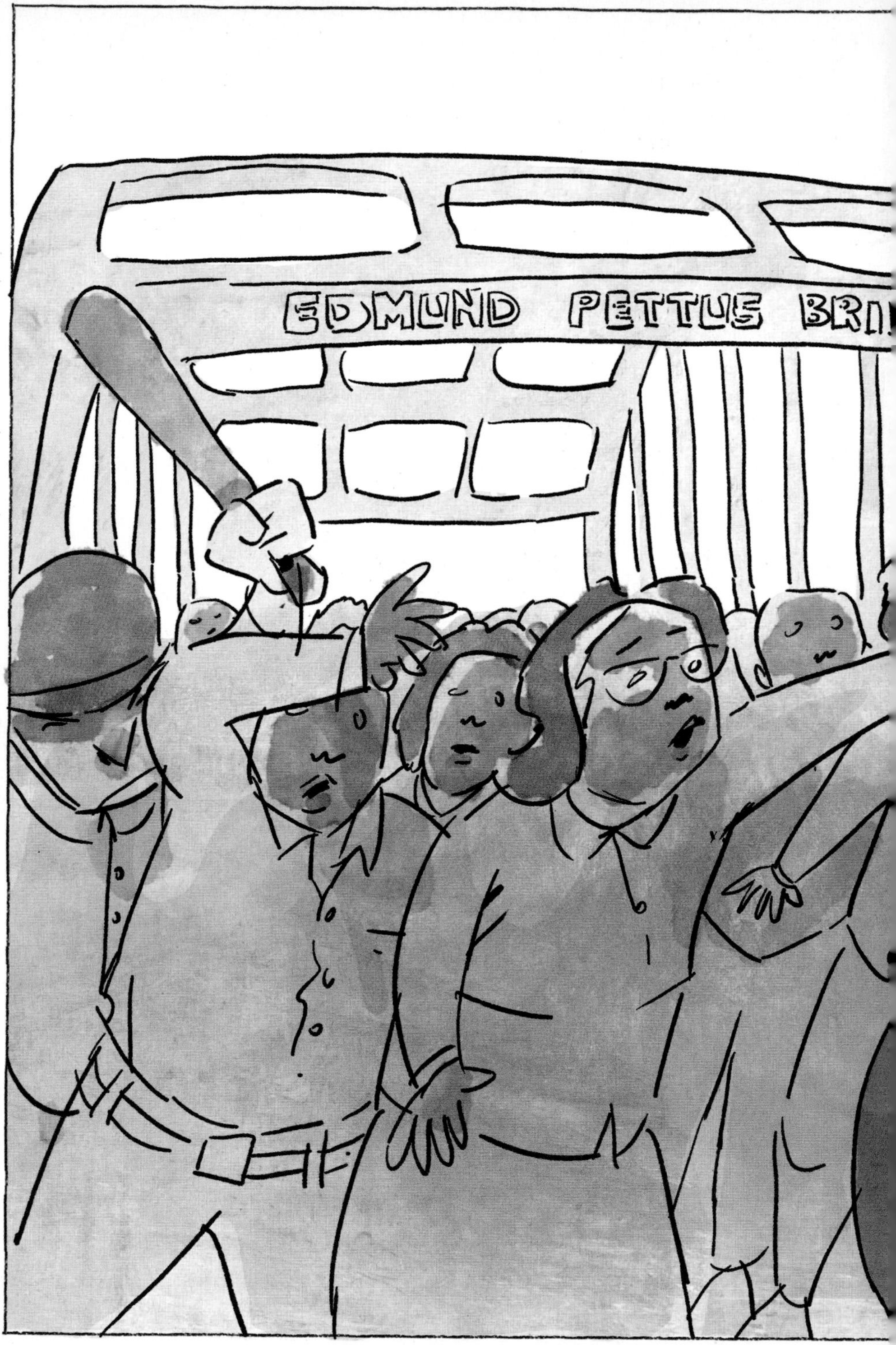
EDMUND PETTUS BRI

Efforts to sweep away Jim Crow quickened in the 1960s: rallies, marches, boycotts, sit-ins, lawsuits. They were met with beatings, bombings, and shootings.

Protesting for civil rights had a price: broken bones, cracked skulls . . . death.

CIVIL RIGHTS ACTIVIST JOHN LEWIS

On August 28, 1963, the Reverend Martin Luther King addressed a crowd of 230,000 that had marched on Washington in support of Civil Rights. King, a leader of that Movement, shared his hopes and dreams.

He echoed Jefferson's towering truth . . .

". . . that all men are created equal."

He saw a future where people would be measured by their character and not their race, a future where people of all races, religions, and nationalities could celebrate in common freedom and the Big Idea of Democracy.

The majesty of King's words matched Jefferson's in the Declaration of Independence, but, like Jefferson's, they voiced more hope than fact.

The blessings of liberty in full and for all still awaits, and among those who await them are Black people, women, Mexican Americans, Latinx Americans, Asian Americans, and members of the LGBTQ+ community.

The Big Idea—a Perfect Union—is unfinished, a grand tower wanting completion, its timbers forever being thrown up, then torn down, just to be remade once more, the work of ever-hopeful builders—we the people.

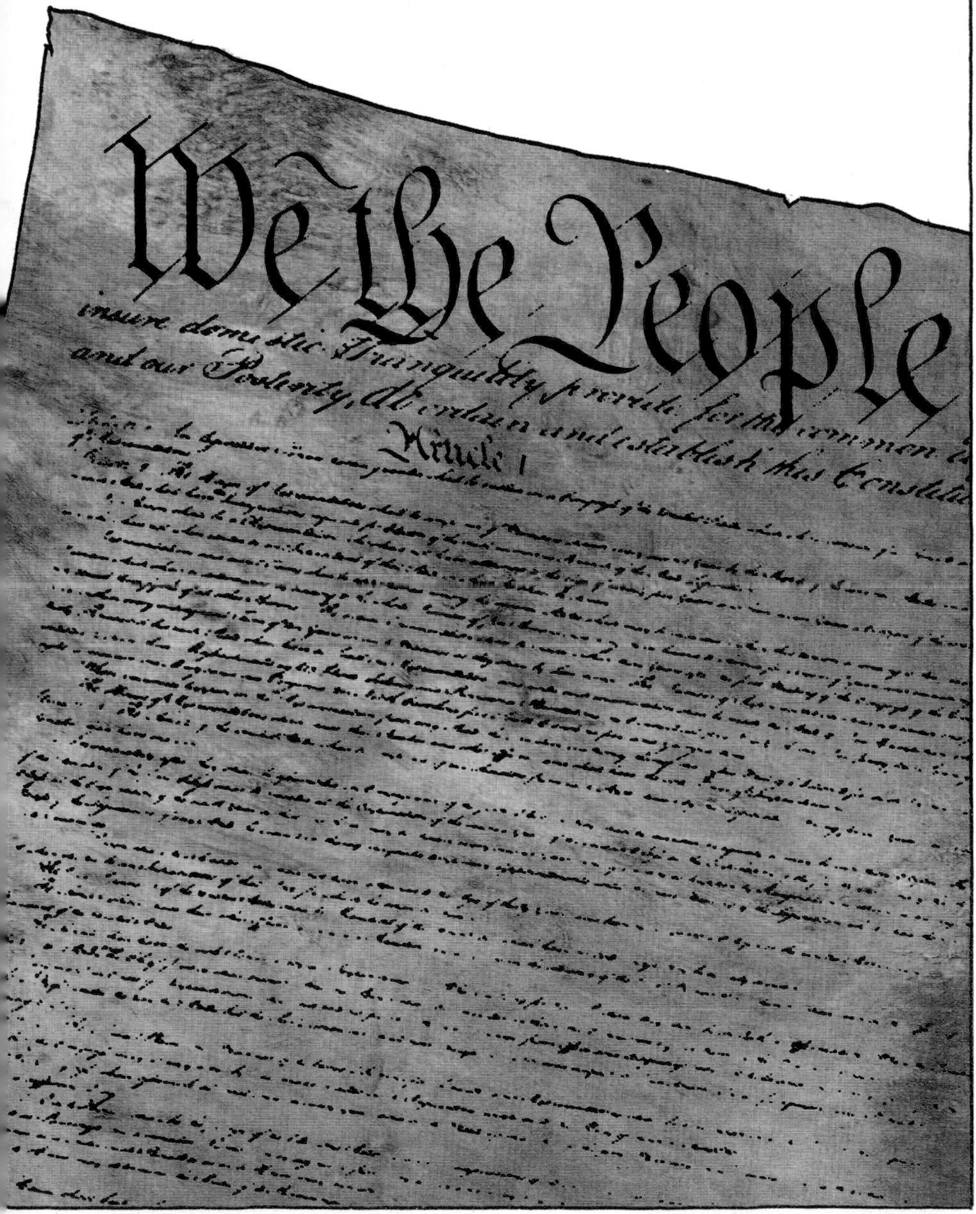
We the People

SELECT TIMELINE

Many dates are approximate.

10000 BCE
Neolithic Revolution. Birth
of farming. Domestication of plants
(wheat and barley). Domestication
of sheep, cattle, water buffalo.

4000 BCE
Domestication of oxen,
donkeys, and camels.

3150–3130 BCE
Egyptian Empire. Rule by pharaohs.

1755–1750 BCE
Code of Hammurabi. Rules set
down by Hammurabi, a king of the
First Babylonian Empire.

44 BCE
Julius Caesar assassinated.
A series of emperors rule
Rome afterward.

27 BCE–476 CE
Roman Empire.

June 15, 1215
Magna Carta signed.

1235–1255
Sundiata Keita, leader of
the Mali Empire.

1236
Manden Charter. Early constitution
of the Mali Empire, West Africa.

10,000 BCE   2,000 BCE   0

600 BCE–400 CE
Republics in ancient India.

507 BCE
Cleisthenes introduces *demokratia*
(democracy) to Athens, Greece.

221–210 BCE
Qin Shi Huang, first emperor
of unified China.

46 BCE
Julius Caesar made
"dictator for life" of Rome.

1521
Montezuma last Emperor
of Aztecs in Mexico.

1570
Iroquois Confederacy
founded (actual date disputed).

1619
House of Burgesses founded in
Virginia. Africans enslaved
in Virginia.

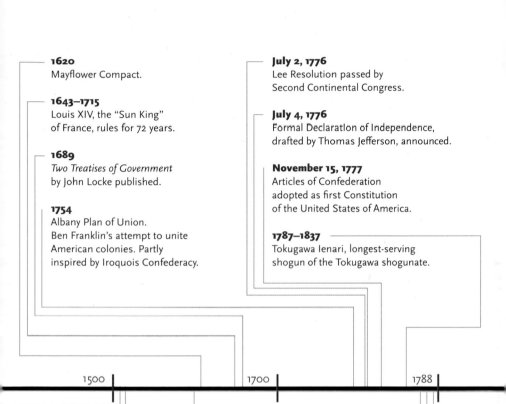

1620
Mayflower Compact.

1643–1715
Louis XIV, the "Sun King"
of France, rules for 72 years.

1689
Two Treatises of Government
by John Locke published.

1754
Albany Plan of Union.
Ben Franklin's attempt to unite
American colonies. Partly
inspired by Iroquois Confederacy.

July 2, 1776
Lee Resolution passed by
Second Continental Congress.

July 4, 1776
Formal Declaration of Independence,
drafted by Thomas Jefferson, announced.

November 15, 1777
Articles of Confederation
adopted as first Constitution
of the United States of America.

1787–1837
Tokugawa Ienari, longest-serving
shogun of the Tokugawa shogunate.

1500   1700   1788

1762–1796
Catherine the Great, empress
regnant of Russia. Longest-
ruling female leader of Russia.

June 7, 1776
Lee Resolution presented by
Richard Henry Lee of Virginia
to Second Continental Congress
proposing American independence
from Great Britain.

June 12, 1776
Virginia Declaration of Rights written
by George Mason is adopted.

May 25, 1787
Constitutional Convention
begins in Philadelphia.

September 17, 1787
Thirty-nine delegates
sign the new, proposed
Constitution. Three decline.

June 21, 1788
A ninth state, New Hampshire,
approves the Constitution,
ensuring its ratification.

1789
First representatives, senators, vice president (John Adams), and president (George Washington) are elected.

1790
Rhode Island becomes the last state to ratify the Constitution.

1792–1804
French depose King Louis XVI and form a republic.

1804
Napoleon seizes power and replaces the First French Republic with the First French Empire.

1860–1865
American Civil War.

December 6, 1865
Thirteenth Amendment ending slavery ratified.

July 28, 1868
Fourteenth Amendment guaranteeing equal justice ratified.

February 3, 1870
Fifteenth Amendment guaranteeing the right to vote ratified.

1872
In Missouri, Virginia Minor denied a vote in presidential election.

1789   1850

1804
Enslaved people of Haiti revolt against the French, claim independence, and create a republic.

1848
Seneca Falls Convention. Women demand the right to vote.

1857
Supreme Court rules against Dred Scott's freedom.

1874
U.S. Supreme Court denies Virginia Minor, and all women, the right to vote.

1896
Supreme Court approves segregation—the legal separation of Black and white people—under a policy known as "Separate but Equal."

1877–1965 (approx.)
Jim Crow laws across the South restrict African Americans' political rights and economic opportunities.

1917
The Seventeenth Amendment
mandates the direct election of
U.S. senators. Jeannette Rankin
of Montana, first woman elected
to U.S. House of Representatives.

1920
Nineteenth Amendment gives
women the right to vote.

1924
Snyder Act passed, making Native
Americans U.S. citizens and giving
them the right to vote.

August 28, 1963
Martin Luther King Jr. gives
"I Have a Dream" speech.

1964
Civil Rights Act passes to destroy
remaining Jim Crow laws.

1965
Voting Rights Act passes to ensure
voting rights of African Americans.

1967
Thurgood Marshall becomes first
Black justice on the Supreme Court.

1900   1950   2020

1932
Hattie Ophelia Wyatt of Arkansas, first
woman elected to U.S. Senate.

1942–1945
Many Japanese Americans are
imprisoned during World War II.

1954
Brown v. Board of Education,
Topeka, Kansas. Supreme Court
finds "separate but equal" laws are
unconstitutional.

1981
Sandra Day O'Connor becomes first
woman justice on the Supreme Court.

2009
Sonia Sotomayor becomes
first Hispanic justice on the
Supreme Court.

2013
United States Supreme Court
strikes down key elements of
1965 Voting Rights Act.

WHO WAS
ABIGAIL ADAMS?

Abigail Adams, portrait painted in 1766 by Benjamin Blythe

Abigail Adams was the wife of John Adams, one of the chief architects of American independence and the new United States republic. He was the first vice president and the second president, making Abigail the first Second Lady and the second First Lady. She was also the mother of the sixth American president, John Quincy Adams. But she is better remembered for her powerful intellect, pithy observations of public life, and keen political instincts.

Abigail "would have been a better president than her husband," said President Harry Truman, a remarkable and admiring comment about someone without a formal education.

Schooling had been denied Abigail simply because she was a girl, but she was not one to be denied. She read the books in the library of her father, a Congregational church pastor, making herself one of the best-read women of her time. We are left to wonder how sharp her intellect could have been had it been polished by a first-class education. Having a front-row seat to a great turn in American history, Abigail has left us with vivid observations of the times.

Of England's King George's difficulties with his colonists, she wrote ". . . a people may let a king fall, yet still remain a people, but if a king let his people slip from him, he is no longer a king."

She saw the contradiction of fighting for American freedom while maintaining homegrown slavery. She wrote "I wish most sincerely that there was not a slave in the province. It always appeared a most iniquitous scheme to me—fight ourselves for what we are daily robbing and plundering from those who have as good a right to freedom as we have."

A victim of the misogynist impulses of her time, she encouraged her husband to promote the rights of women, writing "Remember the Ladies, and be more generous and favorable to them than your ancestors."

John Adams understood the treasure he had in Abigail.

"I want to hear you think or see your thoughts," he wrote, voicing a sentiment we can all share.

NOTES

Page 6—"could we . . . trace them . . . we'd find . . . them nothing better than the principal ruffian of some restless gang." Paine, *Common Sense.*

Page 7—"All men would be tyrants if they could!" National Archives: Founders Online, "Abigail Adams to John Adams."

Page 9—"If a man knock out the teeth of his equal, his teeth shall be knocked out." L.W. King, "The Code of Hammurabi."

Page 12—"You are the son of god . . . your commands, like the word of god cannot be reversed." Duiker and Spielvogel, p. 13.

Page 20—"It is the will of God!" Parker, p. 198.

Page 33—"The state of nature . . . teaches all mankind . . . that being all equal and independent, no one ought to harm another in his life, health, liberty, or possessions . . ." Locke, *Second Treatise of Government.*

Page 37—"It would be a very strange Thing, if six nations of ignorant Savages should be capable of forming a . . . Union . . . yet . . . a (similar) union should be impracticable for ten or a Dozen English Colonies." Little, "The Native American Government that Inspired the U.S. Constitution."

Page 38—"There is something absurd in supposing a continent to be perpetually governed by and island." Lepore, *The Story of America,* 61.

Page 40—"these United Colonies are, and of right ought to be, free and independent States." Lepore, *These Truths,* 98.

Page 41—"We hold these truths to be self-evident, that all men are created equal, that they are endowed by their Creator with certain unalienable Rights, that among these are Life, Liberty and the pursuit of Happiness.–That to secure these rights, Governments are instituted among Men, deriving their just powers from the consent of the governed." National Archives: America's Founding Documents, Declaration of Independence, a Transcription.

Page 42—"That all men are by nature equally free and independent, and have certain inherent rights . . . namely, the enjoyment of life and liberty, with the means of acquiring and possessing property, and pursuing and obtaining happiness and safety." Schwartz, "George Mason, Forgotten Founder, He Conceived the Bill of Rights."

Page 43—"The colonists greeted it with cheers, bells, and cannons. The American Revolution was *on!*" Lepore, *These Truths,* p. 99.

Page 44—"standard against which to measure the nation again and again." Ricks, p. 131.

Page 44—". . . have in Common with all other men a Natural and unalienable Right to that freedom which the Great Parent of the Universe hath Bestowed equally on all mankind." Allen, "A Forgotten Black Founding Father."

Page 49—"Thirteen sovereignties pulling against each other...will soon bring ruin on the whole." Bowen, p. 33.

Page 49—"for the sole and express purpose of reviving the Articles of Confederation." Bowen, p. 11.

Page 51—"Let Congress legislate. Let others execute. Let others judge." Morris, p. 136.

Page 55—"were tired of the excesses of democracy," Ellis, pp. 211–212.

Page 56—"Why, then, should . . . Blacks who were property in the South, be in the rule of representation more than cattle and horses of the North?" Morris, p. 207.

Page 61—". . . who have . . . little property, education, or principle." Lepore, *Story of America*, p. 115.

Page 64—"These lawyers, and men of learning, and moneyed men . . . expect to be the managers of the Constitution, and get all the power . . . and then swallow up all us little folks . . . just as the whale swallowed Jonah. This is what I'm afraid of." Ricks, p. 211.

Page 65—"excellencies of republican government might be retained and imperfections lessened or avoided," Morris, p. 228.

Page 65—"A disturbance in Albany, New York . . . occasioned bloodshed." Ricks, p. 215.

Page 69—"The nauseous business of amendment," Ellis, p. 213.

Page 71—"One section of the country believes slavery is right and ought to be extended, while the other believes it is wrong and ought not to be extended." Lepore, *Story of America*, p. 316.

Page 73—". . . no rights which the white man was bound to respect; and that the negro might justly and lawfully be reduced to slavery for his benefit. (Black people could be) bought and sold and treated as an ordinary article of merchandise . . ." PBS.org, "Africans in America: Dred Scott case: the Supreme Court decision."

Page 74—". . . it is too clear for dispute, that the enslaved African race were not intended to be included . . ." PBS.org, "Dred Scott case."

Page 79—"I walked out (of slavery) like a man and shouldered my responsibilities." Foner, "South Carolina's Forgotten Black Political Revolution."

Page 80—". . . we hold this to be a Government of White People, made and to be perpetuated for the exclusive benefit of the White race, and . . . that the people of African descent cannot be considered as citizens of the United States." Staff of the Klanwatch Project of the Southern Poverty Law Center, "Ku Klux Klan: A History of Racism and Violence."

Page 83—"We hold these truths to be self-evident; that all men *and women* are created equal . . ." National Archives: America's Founding Documents, "Declaration of Independence, a Transcription."

Page 83—Women were too "delicate," too "impulsive and excitable" to vote. Parkman, "The Woman Question."

Page 83—And besides, "You do not need a ballot to clean out your sink." Pamphlet of the National Association Opposed to Woman Suffrage, National Women's History Museum.

Page 87—"Constitution of the United States does not confer the right of suffrage (that is, the right to vote) upon anyone." *Minor v. Happersett.*

Page 93—"[Women] . . . will not hold ourselves bound by any laws in which we have no voice or representation." National Archives: Founders Online, "Abigail Adams to John Adams, 31 March 1776."

Page 97—"Separate educational facilities are inherently unequal." National Park Service, "1954: Brown v. Board of Education."

Page 103—"I have a dream that one day this nation . . ." King Jr., "I Have a Dream: Full Text March on Washington Speech."

SELECTED BIBLIOGRAPHY

Primary Sources

Bradford, William, et al. "Mayflower Compact, 1620." Avalon Project, Yale Law School. See liberalarts.utexas.edu/coretexts/_files/resources/texts/1620%20Mayflower%20 Compact.pdf.

Legal Information Institute, Cornell Law School. *Minor v. Happersett*. See www.law.cornell. edu/supremecourt/text/88/162.

Library of Congress: Research Guides. "Full Text of the Federalist Papers," nos. 51–60. See guides.loc.gov/federalist-papers/text-51-60.

———. "Kansas-Nebraska Act: Primary Documents in American History." See guides.loc. gov/kansas-nebraska-act.

———. "Missouri Compromise: Primary Documents in American History." See guides. loc.gov/missouri-compromise.

Massachusetts Historical Society. "Letter from Abigail Adams to John Adams, 22 September 1774." See www.masshist.org/digitaladams/archive/doc?id=L17740922aa.

National Archives: America's Founding Documents. "Declaration of Independence, a History." See www.archives.gov/founding-docs/declaration-history.

———. "Declaration of Independence, a Transcription." See www.archives.gov/founding-docs/declaration-transcript.

———. "The Constitution: A History." See www.archives.gov/founding-docs/more-perfect-union.

———. "The Constitution: How Did It Happen?" See www.archives.gov/founding-docs/constitution/how-did-it-happen.

———. "The Constitution: How Was It Made?" See www.archives.gov/founding-docs/constitution/how-was-it-made.

National Archives: Founders Online. "Abigail Adams to John Adams, 31 March 1776." See founders.archives.gov/documents/Adams/04-01-02-0241.

National Archives: The Center for Legislative Archives. "17th Amendment to the Constitution: Direct Election of Senators." See www.archives.gov/legislative/features/17th-amendment.

National Park Service. "1954: *Brown v. Board of Education*." See www.nps.gov/articles/brown-v-board-of-education.htm.

———. "Abigail Adams (1744–1818)." See www.nps.gov/adam/learn/historyculture/abigail-adams-1744-1818.htm.

———. "Birth of the Civil Rights Movement, 1941–1954." See www.nps.gov/subjects/civil-rights/birth-of-civil-rights.htm.

———. "Jim Crow Laws." See www.nps.gov/malu/learn/education/jim_crow_laws.htm.

United States House of Representatives: History, Art, and Archives. "Blanche Kelso Bruce." See history.house.gov/People/Detail/10029.

———. "Delegates of the Continental and Confederation Congresses Who Signed the United States Constitution." See history.house.gov/People/Continental-Congress/Signatories.

Yale Law School, Avalon Project. "Mayflower Compact." See avalon.law.yale.edu/17th_century/mayflower.asp.

———. "Magna Carta 1215." See avalon.law.yale.edu/medieval/magframe.asp.

Books

Allison, Robert J., and Bernard Bailyn, eds. *The Essential Debate on the Constitution*. New York: Library of America, 2018.

Arrian and Chinnock, E. J., trans. *The Anabasis of Alexander, Books 5–7*. Cambridge, MA: Harvard University Press, 1983. See en.wikisource.org/wiki/The_Anabasis_of_Alexander/Book_V/Chapter_I.

Bowen, Catherine Drinker. *Miracle at Philadelphia*. Boston: Little Brown and Company, 1986.

Brookhiser, Richard. *James Madison*. New York: Basic Books, 2011.

Cooke, Alistair. *Alistair Cooke's America*. New York: Knopf, 1973.

Duiker, William J., and Jackson J. Spielvogel. *World History*, ninth ed. Boston: Cengage, 2019.

Ellis, Joseph J. *The Quartet: Orchestrating the Second American Revolution, 1783–1789*. New York: Knopf, 2015.

Feldman, Noah. *The Three Lives of James Madison*. New York: Random House, 2017.

Gelles, Edith B. *Abigail & John*. New York: HarperCollins, 2009.

Klarman, Michael J. *The Framers' Coup: The Making of the United States Constitution*. New York: Oxford University Press, 2016.

Kwarteng, Kwasi. *War and Gold*. New York: PublicAffairs, 2014.

Lepore, Jill. *These Truths: A History of the United States*. New York: W.W. Norton, 2018.

———. *The Story of America*. Princeton, NJ: Princeton University Press, 2012.

Locke, John. *Second Treatise of Government*. Indianapolis, IN: Hackett Publishing, 1980. See www.gutenberg.org/files/7370/7370-h/7370-h.htm.

McCullough, David. *John Adams*. New York: Simon & Schuster, 2001.

McDonald, Forrest. *Novus Ordo Seclorum: The Intellectual Origins of the Constitution*. Lawrence, KS: University Press of Kansas, 1985.

Morris, Richard B. *Witnesses at the Creation*. New York: New American Library, 1986.

Paine, Thomas. *Common Sense*. See archive.org/details/commonsense00painrich/page/30/mode/2up?ref=ol&view=theater.

————. The Project Gutenberg eBook of Common Sense. Philadelphia: W. & T. Bradford, 1776. See www.gutenberg.org/files/147/147-h/147-h.htm#thoughts.

Parker, Philip. *World History*. New York: DK Publishing, 2010.

Ricks, Thomas E. *First Principles: What the Founding Fathers Learned from the Greeks and Romans and How That Shaped Our Country*. New York: HarperCollins, 2002.

Wolfe, James and Favor, Lesli J. *Understanding the Iroquois Constitution*. New York: Enslow Publishing, 2015.

Articles

Allen, Danielle. "A Forgotten Black Founding Father." *Atlantic*, March 2021. See www.theatlantic.com/magazine/archive/2021/03/prince-hall-forgotten-founder/617791.

————. "The Declaration's Dual Traditions: Broad Equality, and Equality for Whites." *Washington Post,* July 2, 2015. See www.washingtonpost.com/opinions/a-declaration-of-conflicts/2015/07/02/6e2f93c4-2021-11e5-aeb9-a411a84c9d55_story.html.

————. "The Flawed Genius of the Constitution." *Atlantic*, October 2020. See www.theatlantic.com/magazine/archive/2020/10/danielle-allen-constitution/615481.

Al-Mohamed, Day. "Gouverneur Morris: Playboy and Penman of the American Constitution." *American Masters*, PBS, November 11, 2020. See www.pbs.org/wnet/americanmasters/blog/gouverneur-morris-playboy-and-penman-of-the-american-constitution.

Andrews, Evan. "Seven Influential African Empires." History.com, August 22, 2018. See www.history.com/news/7-influential-african-empires.

Annenberg Classroom. "Civil Rights Act of 1875 Struck Down." Annenberg Public Policy Center. See www.annenbergclassroom.org/timeline_event/civil-rights-act-of-1875-declared-unconstitutional.

BBC History. "Catherine the Great (1729–1796)." See www.bbc.co.uk/history/historic_figures/catherine_the_great.shtml.

————. "George III (1738–1820.)" See www.bbc.co.uk/history/historic_figures/george_iii_king.shtml.

Canadian War Museum. "New France and the Iroquois Wars." See www.warmuseum.ca/cwm/exhibitions/chrono/1000iroquois_e.html.

Center for the Study of the American Constitution, University of Wisconsin. "Constitutional Convention." See csac.history.wisc.edu/document-collections/the-constitutional-convention.

Child, John Brown. "On the Peace Road? Some Reflections on 9/11." Centro de Investigaciones sobre América del Norte, Universidad de Guadalajara, February 2, 2007. See www.cisan.unam.mx/Speaking/Speaking/John%20Brown.pdf.

Connecticut History.org. "The Connecticut Compromise—Today in History: July 16." See connecticuthistory.org/the-connecticut-compromise.

DuBois, Ellen. "Reconstruction and the Battle for Woman Suffrage." Gilder Lehrman Institute of American History. See www.gilderlehrman.org/history-resources/essays/reconstruction-and-battle-woman-suffrage.

Edwards, Rebecca. "Early Woman's Rights Activists Wanted More Than Suffrage." History.com, April 1, 2019. See www.history.com/news/early-womens-rights-movement-beyond-suffrage.

Foner, Eric. "South Carolina's Forgotten Black Political Revolution." *Slate*, January 31, 2018. See slate.com/human-interest/2018/01/the-many-black-americans-who-held-public-office-during-reconstruction-in-southern-states-like-south-carolina.html.

———. "Reconstruction." National Parks Service. See www.nps.gov/articles/reconstruction.htm.

Hannah-Jones, Nikole, creator. "The 1619 Project." *New York Times Magazine*, August 18, 2019. See archive.org/details/1619project/full_issue_of_the_1619_project/page/n3/mode/2up.

Hansen, Terri. "How the Iroquois Great Law of Peace Shaped U.S. Democracy." Native Voices Blog, PBS, December 17, 2018. See www.pbs.org/native-america/blogs/native-voices/how-the-iroquois-great-law-of-peace-shaped-us-democracy.

History.com editors. "Abigail Adams Urges Husband to 'Remember the Ladies.'" History.com, October 22, 2009. See www.history.com/this-day-in-history/abigail-adams-urges-husband-to-remember-the-ladies.

———. "America's History of Slavery Began Long Before Jamestown." History.com, August 26, 2019. See www.history.com/news/american-slavery-before-jamestown-1619.

———. "Ancient Greek Democracy." History.com, August 19, 2019. See www.history.com/topics/ancient-greece/ancient-greece-democracy.

———. "Ancient Rome." History.com, August 19, 2019. See www.history.com/topics/ancient-rome/ancient-rome.

———. "Articles of Confederation." History.com, September 27, 2019. See www.history.com/topics/early-us/articles-of-confederation.

———. "Aztecs." History.com, September 9, 2020. See www.history.com/topics/ancient-americas/aztecs.

———. "Compromise of 1850." History.com, February 10, 2020. See www.history.com/topics/abolitionist-movement/compromise-of-1850.

———. "Hunter-Gatherers." History.com, January 5, 2018. See www.history.com/topics/pre-history/hunter-gatherers.

———. "I Have a Dream." History.com, March 16, 2021. See www.history.com/topics/civil-rights-movement/i-have-a-dream-speech.

———. "Jamestown Colony." History.com, August 28, 2020, See www.history.com/topics/colonial-america/jamestown.

———. "Little Rock Nine." History.com, February 10, 2020. See www.history.com/topics/black-history/central-high-school-integration

———. "Louis XIV." History.com, October 9, 2019. See www.history.com/topics/france/louis-xiv.

———. "Magna Carta." History.com, September 20, 1919. See www.history.com/topics/british-history/magna-carta.

———. "Nineteenth Amendment 1920." History.com, February 25, 2021. See www.history.com/topics/womens-history/19th-amendment-1.

———. "Plessy versus Ferguson." History.com, January 20, 2021. See www.history.com/topics/black-history/plessy-v-ferguson.

Independence Hall Association. "City Tavern." USHistory.org. See www.ushistory.org/tour/city-tavern.htm.

Khan, Syed Muhammad. "Islamic Caliphates." *World History Encyclopedia*, December 3, 2019. See www.ancient.eu/Islamic_Caliphates.

Kimberly, Maria. "House of Burgesses." George Washington's Mount Vernon. See www.mountvernon.org/library/digitalhistory/digital-encyclopedia/article/house-of-burgesses.

King, L. W., trans. "The Code of Hammurabi." Avalon Project, Yale Law School. See avalon.law.yale.edu/ancient/hamframe.asp.

King Jr., Martin Luther. "I Have a Dream: Full Text March on Washington Speech." NAACP. See www.naacp.org/i-have-a-dream-speech-full-march-on-washington.

Klanwatch Project of the Southern Poverty Law Center. "Ku Klux Klan: A History of Racism and Violence." March 1, 2011. See www.splcenter.org/20110228/ku-klux-klan-history-racism.

Martin Luther King Jr. Research and Education Institute, Stanford University. "Assassination of Martin Luther King Jr." See kinginstitute.stanford.edu/encyclopedia/assassination-martin-luther-king-jr.

Lange, Allison. "National Association Opposed to Women's Suffrage." National Women's History Museum. See www.crusadeforthevote.org/naows-opposition.

Little, Becky. "The Native American Government that Inspired the U.S. Constitution." History.com, November 8, 2020. See www.history.com/news/iroquois-confederacy-influence-us-constitution.

———. "Who Was Jim Crow?" *National Geographic*, August 6, 2015. See www.nationalgeographic.com/history/article/150806-voting-rights-act-anniversary-jim-crow-segregation-discrimination-racism-history.

Muhlberger, Steve. "Democracy in Ancient India." Nipissing University, 1998. See www.infinityfoundation.com/mandala/h_es/h_es_muhlb_democra.htm.

Murphy, Gerald. "About the Iroquois Constitution." Fordham University, 1998. See sourcebooks.fordham.edu/mod/iroquois.asp.

National Geographic. "The Mali Empire." See www.nationalgeographic.org/encyclopedia/mali-empire.

Paine, Thomas. "Common Sense" (excerpt). Thomas Paine Society. See www.thomaspainesociety.org/common-sense.

Parkman, Francis. "The Woman Question." *North American Review*, October 1879. See www.jstor.org/stable/pdf/25100797.pdf.

PBS.org. "Africans in America: Dred Scott Case—The Supreme Court Decision." See www.pbs.org/wgbh/aia/part4/4h2933.html.

———. "American Experience: Ku Klux Klan in the 1920s." See www.pbs.org/wgbh/americanexperience/features/flood-klan.

———. "Japan: Memoirs of a Secret Empire." See www.pbs.org/empires/japan/timeline_1700.html.

Schwartz, Steven A. "George Mason, Forgotten Founder: He Conceived the Bill of Rights." *Smithsonian Magazine*, April 30, 2000. See www.smithsonianmag.com/history/george-mason-forgotten-founder-he-conceived-the-bill-of-rights-64408583.

The Standard. "The Mande Charter (*Kouroukan Fouga*) of 1235." June 2, 2014. See standard.gm/mande-charter-kouroukan-fouga-1235.

Teachingamericanhistory.com. "Day-to-Day Summary of the Convention." See teachingamericanhistory.org/resources/convention/summary.

UNESCO. "Manden Charter, proclaimed in Kurukan Fuga." See ich.unesco.org/en/RL/manden-charter-proclaimed-in-kurukan-fuga-00290.

Video

PBS.org. *Haudenosaunee's Legendary Founding*. August 15, 2018. See www.pbs.org/video/haudenosaunees-legendary-founding-ziahzz.

AUTHOR'S NOTE

"Many forms of Government have been tried . . . No one pretends that democracy is perfect or all-wise. Indeed, it has been said that democracy is the worst form of Government except for all those other(s) . . ." Winston Churchill's words remain as pithy today as when he first uttered them in 1947. We consider the Greeks to have invented democracy, the astonishing and novel idea of governance by the people. (Perhaps there was an earlier group of progressive thinkers, but if so they didn't have the good sense to write the idea down.) But the Greeks were only able to maintain democracy for a couple hundred years before it sank beneath the waves of kingly rule. Then the Romans gave a version of democracy a spin but let it collapse under the weight of tyrants. For about the next two thousand years, the world knew mostly kings and queens and princes and shoguns and sultans and other manner of one-person rule, nearly all of them insisting this was God's idea.

Then at the close of the eighteenth century, plucky Americans—gaga for everything Greek and Roman—decided democracy was just the thing for their newly independent republic. Not direct, Greek-style democracy where everyone had a say; the Founding Fathers were cold to the idea that people less educated and less rich than themselves should be given much power. They believed American democracy should be *representational*, that is, ordinary people choosing smarter and richer others to represent them in the business of governing.

Of course, for the first two hundred years, the blessings of democracy would fall mainly on white men and be merely a promise for everyone else, but that promise alone was enough to inspire a quickening of democracy in the twentieth century. That century saw the First World War—a spasm of violence between cousin-kings, the Second World War—a defeat of tyrannical, fascist genocide, the rejection of the colonial system, and the collapse of Soviet domination. Places newly unshackled chose democracy as the path forward for national stability and success.

Today more than half the world lives in a democracy, some more flawed than others, but democracies nonetheless. Still, wide stretches of the globe—China, Russia, and parts of Africa, for starters—are not democratic. Democracy's history isn't one of long life, and the eternal struggle for all those who practice it is to "hold on." Economic distress and racial and ethnic tensions breed political turmoil and dissatisfaction. Confidence in the very *rightness* of democracy can corrode. The guarantee of equal justice can fade. Unfettered voting rights can wither. The United States is clearly not immune to these afflictions.

America's democracy is the world's oldest.

How will it age?

INDEX